WELCOME TO THE DARKSIDE

A BDSM PRIMER

SECOND EDITION

RAJAN DOMINARI

WELCOME TO THE DARKSIDE

A BDSM PRIMER

SECOND EDITION

A PRACTICAL GUIDE TO HELP YOU
BEGIN YOUR JOURNEY IN DISCOVERING
BDSM AND KINK

RAVEN ROW PRESS

R.

Published by Raven Row Press

This is a work of non-fiction, written to offer encouragement, mentorship, and practical guidance to those navigating Dominant/submissive relationships. The views expressed reflect the author's personal insights and lived experience, and are intended for informational and inspirational purposes only. This book is not a substitute for professional, medical, psychological, or legal advice.

Revised and expanded edition © 2025 by Rajan Dominari
ISBN (Paperback): 978-1-7345271-6-2

Cover design, interior artwork and layout: Studio Pedroza

Printed and published in the United States of America

For Dominant Desires-specific inquiries, contact:
domdesiresofficial@gmail.com

For permissions, inquiries, or bulk orders, please contact:
Raven Row Press
ravenrow@akopublishing.com

DEDICATION

To my uncle for being an amazing mentor, and for seeing something in me I would've never dreamed existed. To the elder members of my house, all for being great leaders and lending a part of who I am today. To my Six, for being a group of the most fantastic submissives I could've ever asked for.

To my mum for being half the reason I exist, and for being my biggest fan. My dad for showing me that to love someone without equivocation is an awesome thing in the right hands.

And finally to my granddad for being one of the biggest influences in my life, for always showing me how gentleman rules always apply to every aspect of life from business to basic courtesy, and teaching me how to use them. I'll always be grateful that you ever existed, and I couldn't have asked for a better grandfather.

FOREWORD

When I first released Welcome to the Darkside, my goal was to offer a grounded, real-world guide for anyone starting their journey into BDSM. Over the years, I've heard from readers all over the world—and this updated version reflects some of that shared experience, reader feedback, and the continued growth of the communities this book was written for.

This revised edition smooths out a few of the original's rough spots and refreshes the layout for easier reading. You'll also find a few new sections, reworded passages, re-imagined artwork, and cleaner phrasing that sharpen the book's voice.

The heart of the book remains the same—but it speaks more clearly now.

Whether this is your first time reading or you're coming back to it after some time—thank you. It means a lot knowing this book found its way into your hands, and hopefully, deepens your understanding of yourself, your dynamic, and this lifestyle.

— Rajan Dominari, 2025

TABLE OF CONTENTS

PRAISE FOR WELCOME TO THE DARKSIDE: A BDSM PRIMER

Dominari has written one of the ultimate books on BDSM, kink, and D/s relationships ... For me, there was nothing dark about Welcome to the Darkside. I was enlightened and found tools to apply in my personal D/s relationship.

Munson, Illinois

The book Christian Grey should've taken lessons from. Definitely a must-read.

Evan, London

One of the few original BDSM people who is honest and helpful. Not only does Rajan help educate people about BDSM, he doesn't mainstream it. He helps newcomers in an honest form. His writing style is entertaining and truly insightful.

Amber, Utah

I highly recommend this book to anyone who needs factual information instead of most of the crap that's out there... Everything I've read or heard by Rajan Dominari has helped undo a lot of damage for me.

Angie, Goodreads Reviewer

I first met Rajan Dominari in mid-2019 as a newbie submissive looking for guidance ... He wasn't just anybody—he was a Master, someone who could write a bible to BDSM. Rajan is the real deal; all that flows from his mouth is honesty, and he's not afraid to tell the wannabes where to stick it ... I hadn't purchased one book until I came across Welcome to the Darkside. I now consider him a mentor and a friend from afar.

Naomi, Texas

If you're new to the lifestyle or you've been in it for a while, Welcome to the Darkside is definitely a book worth picking up and reading. It's helped me better my knowledge of our lifestyle not only for myself, but for my partner/submissive as well.

Dominique, New Mexico

Welcome to the Darkside is a great book for both newbies and experts alike. Always great to refer back to and to keep on hand. Rajan really knows his stuff and will always be a great part of this beautiful community.

Rachel, New Mexico

Rajan's writing has allowed me to have a clear vision of BDSM, of the link that there could be between a master and his submissive, the mutual respect to have, and the rules to respect. I built myself with them, and today I share some of his words with my master when I send him a message to tell him how I'm doing. It's a shame that Rajan is so far away. I think I would have a lot to learn from him!

Flolie, France

I started reading articles from the Dominant Desires website when I revisited my desire to learn more about BDSM. Rajan Dominari's articles helped build my confidence and expanded my way of thinking. His expertise helped me create an outline for what to expect from a partner and a relationship. His writings are informative and candid, and his humor is the icing on the cake! Welcome to the Darkside is a fantastic read!

Mackenzie, South Carolina

Rajan has really helped me understand more about the roles and what role you are more comfortable as. Whether it be a submissive or Dominant.

Sin, West Virginia

I have read Rajan's writings on FetLife, listened to his podcast, and read his book. Not stalking, but all of them have helped on my journey in this lifestyle. He has a unique voice which I enjoy, he breaks topics down so they are easy to grasp, and the words make the reader feel like it's a conversation with a friend, not a lecture or dissertation on the various aspects of BDSM like some of the other books out there. I look forward to reading and hearing more from him.

littleredheadBBW, California

Rajan's posts made me see that not every decent master has to be a pathetic asshole. One who thinks of his pleasure alone. His posts made me see the fun part of BDSM also and got me a genuine interest in ropes, more ropes, and BDSM art.

Sophia, Netherlands

When I was first discovering the lifestyle, it was Rajan's memes that got me thinking outside of my vanilla mind. I had always desired most of the things they said, but never knew how to put it into words until they caught my eye. Then when I was hooked, and wanted to learn more on his podcast which gave me a deeper understanding of different aspects of it all. I'm excited to see what he has to say in his book!

Daisy Girl, Texas

I'm new to the community and have read a few books which tend to be overwhelming and too much information. Welcome to the Darkside is a great, well-written book to give you just enough information to feel confident to step forward.

Nicole, Illinois

AUTHOR'S NOTE

This book wasn't pulled from academic journals or research papers. It's built on years of lived experience, personal memory, and what I've learnt from people who've actually lived this lifestyle—not just written about it.

Most of what you'll read was passed down through mentors, scenes, conversations, and the shared wisdom of the Dominants and submissives in my community. Some of it comes from experiences I've had with people from other communities over the years. Everything else, I figured out the hard way.

Now, I'm not claiming this is the only way. It's just *my* way— collected, tested, and refined over time. If it helps you, great. If not, toss it. Either way, I appreciate you taking the time to check this book out. Just know: what you're reading comes from a place of experience, not theory.

Welcome to the Darkside. I think you'll like it here.

— *Rajan*

INTRODUCTION

You know, I'd always wanted to write a book, but I honestly never really got around to doing it. Mainly because I'm REALLY good at procrastinating when I don't feel like doing something. So instead of writing a book—which I thought would be absolutely knackering—I started a website. You may have heard of it, actually. It's called Dominant Desires. I initially made the website so I could bitch about the problems I was seeing within the BDSM lifestyle. But then I started answering questions about things within this lifestyle that a lot of people were having problems finding answers to. I thought that it would do people a bit of good, because I have my own particular way of speaking on the subject. However, I did eventually get around to writing a book—and here we are.

To be fair, it took a long time for me to actually get around to writing this book. But I've already begun typing, and believe it or not, I'm actually writing this in joggers, in desperate need of a shower. I'm pretty sure you didn't need to know that. But fuck it, it's been shared now. Deal with it.

The reason I'm writing this book is because everybody has their own take on BDSM. Seriously, if you take a look at any particular book out there, you'll see that everyone is saying something different, whilst simultaneously saying the exact same thing. Because of this, I've decided that I'm going to throw my hat into the ring. To be honest, I had initially thought that I was going to just come out and start tossing out a bunch of information on BDSM, but I ultimately decided that it would be kind of stupid of me to do so, given the possibility that a lot of you reading this book may not have even read anything that I've ever written before.

So I'm going to take an opportunity to rectify that. The way that

I'm going to do this is by starting from the basics, because solid foundations are an important thing. Now if you're not new to BDSM at all, everything I'm saying will likely seem old hat to you, and really not mean much to you, but I thank you for buying the book anyway. If this is a new journey into BDSM for you, then hopefully something I say will be insightful to you, or educate you in some way.

In any case, if you're reading this, I just want to say thanks. Mainly because I wasn't sure if anyone would want to read a book I wrote. Turns out, a LOT of you did, which makes me kinda glad to know that you trust me enough to educate you about this lifestyle.

Another thing I should say early on is that a lot of this book is directed toward s-types, but any D-type might be able to learn something whilst reading as well.

So, erm... you ready? Let's get started.

' You don't need to understand why it moves you.
You only need to admit that it does'
— *Rajan Dominari*

Chapter 1:

WHAT IS BDSM, ANYWAY?

For some of you, when you hear the letters BDSM, the thought of Rihanna singing about whips and chains, or thoughts of Madonna circa 1990, might come to mind in some way (I'll have you know that Madonna came to my mind a lot when I was a kid). In recent years, what typically comes to mind when people think about BDSM is author E. L. James' *Fifty Shades of Grey* books.

Now it goes without saying that no one who is really involved in this lifestyle is even a fan of the FSoG franchise. However, there is absolutely no denying that the series brought this lifestyle to the eyes of millions. But what is BDSM exactly? I'm going to go ahead and shed some light on this for you.

◇◇◇

What Does BDSM Mean?

So to start, way back in the day, what went on to become BDSM started off as S&M—Sadism and Masochism. Sadism and Masochism were terms coined by German psychiatrist Richard von

Krafft-Ebing, back in the 1800s. I'll explain more about these in a bit.

Now, the term BDSM originated around 1969, being broken into four categories: Bondage, Discipline, Sadism, and Masochism. The categories were later further broken into three divisions: Bondage/Discipline, Domination/Submission, and Sadism/Masochism, which has since become the most widely understood use of the acronym by BDSM practitioners.

Even though early S&M practitioners had slaves that they used for various forms of pleasure for hundreds of years, the addition of the B&D was brought on by books like Pauline Reage's *Histoire d'O*—commonly known as 'Story of O'—published in 1954, and John Norman's *Chronicles of Gor* series, published in 1966.

Bondage is any kind of item used to restrain any part of a submissive or slave's body. The most commonly used restraints are handcuffs, rope, or some type of quick-release or Velcro closing restraint.

Discipline is the actions taken by a Dominant to teach and prevent a submissive from doing something that is in no way an act of wilful disobedience. Discipline doesn't normally include physical punishment.

Sadism describes the experience of taking sexual, mental, or emotional pleasure from inflicting pain, humiliation, degradation, or cruelty on someone, or watching others inflict these behaviours on someone else.

Masochism is a source of sexual, mental, or emotional gratification, or the tendency to derive sexual, mental, or emotional gratification from being physically or emotionally abused.

Nowadays, BDSM has become a sort of umbrella where most, if not all, kinky things fall. It could contain all of the elements I mentioned, or just one of them. It really just depends on the person involved. And if it happens to be that one, or a ton of things that make sense to you, then fan-fucking-tastic. You do you, buckaroo.

With all this said, BDSM is ultimately about two or more people trusting and caring for one another, sometimes expressing this via erotic play sessions. This is one of the reasons I feel that BDSM is so attractive to those who want to become involved with it.

However, too many newbies—especially those whose knowledge of BDSM is derived purely from pornography, or films like Fifty Shades of Grey (ugh)—BDSM probably seems like some sort of warped power dynamic, or even abuse.

Throughout this book, I'm most certainly am going to do my best to knock that completely out of your head. All the beautifully kinky things done in BDSM are done in a way that (should) develop an intimacy between the people involved.

◇◇◇

Sadism, Masochism and Sadomasochism

As I mentioned, German psychiatrist Richard von Krafft-Ebing coined the terms sadism and masochism. He brought the terms into medical terminology in his 1890 work, *Neue Forschungen auf dem Gebiet der Psychopathia Sexualis* ('New Research in the Area of Psychopathology of Sex'). The book spoke of basic, natural tendencies to sadism in men and to masochism in women—which, for the record, says more about his era's gender norms than it does about human psychology.

Over time, sadism, masochism and sadomasochism have become

three words that are often confused. So I'm going to go into a little more detail about the differences between the definitions of the words, where they came from and other random information that will hopefully help you to understand the words better.

What is Sadism?

Sadism is the practice of obtaining pleasure by inflicting pain and suffering on another, with most people feeling sexually turned on by various acts, like watching their partner squirm and wriggle from the metallic bite of a Whartenberg wheel, seeing their skin marked from the stinging whip of a flogger, or the reddened skin left from the cracking of a paddle against their body.

Or in my case, totally freak the fuck out when I use anything involving electricity. Hm, I do love electricity. But moving on...

The reason I said 'with most people' is that sadism may or may not be of a sexual nature. For example, I happen to be a sadist, but I'm not sexually turned on by inflicting pain on anyone. And I can't be the only one who feels this way, you know?

To continue, a person who practices sadism is a sadist, and the adjective form is sadistic. Krafft-Ebing derived the word sadism from Donatien Alphonse François de Sade, better known as the Marquis de Sade. De Sade was an eighteenth-century French nobleman who wrote novels depicting sexual violence and cruelty, of which the best known are 1791's *Justine*, and *Juliette*, which was published in 1797. In most cases, a sadist is usually the Dominant partner in a BDSM relationship.

How delightful are the pleasures of the imagination! In those delectable moments, the whole world is ours; not a single creature resists us, we devastate the world, we repopulate it with new objects which, in turn, we immolate. The means to every crime is ours, and

we employ them all; we multiply the horror a hundredfold.
Marquis de Sade, Les prospérités du vice

What is Masochism?

Masochism is the practice of obtaining pleasure by infliction pain and suffering on oneself. Like sadism, masochism may or may not be of a sexual nature.

A person who practices masochism is a masochist, and the adjective form is masochistic. The word masochism is derived from the name of Austrian author Leopold von Sacher-Masoch, the author of the 1870 novel *Venus in Furs*, a novel depicting sexual submission. One interesting thing to note is that the novel depicted male—not female—submission.

Man is the one who desires, woman the one who is desired. This is woman's entire but decisive advantage. Through man's passions, nature has given man into woman's hands, and the woman who does not know how to make him her subject, her slave, her toy, and how to betray him with a smile in the end is not wise.
Leopold von Sacher-Masoch, Venus in Furs

What is Sadomasochism?

Sadomasochism is the practice of obtaining pleasure by both inflicting pain and having pain inflicted upon oneself. Sadomasochism is typically ALWAYS of a sexual nature. The person who practices sadomasochism is a sadomasochist; the adjective form is sadomasochistic.

The word sadomasochism first appeared in 1913 from Viennese Psychoanalyst Isidor Isaak Sadger, as a combination of the words sadism and masochism. Sadomasochism can be spelt with or without a hyphen, although you'll likely see it spelt with a hyphen as in sado-masochism.

Another thing to note, is that not all Dominants are sadists, and as I mentioned before, not all submissives are masochists. There's absolutely nothing wrong with that, either. There's no rule that says that anyone HAS to be anything. Well, except for Dominants being Dominants, and submissives being submissives. That's kind of a thing, you know?

◇◇◇

Things to Be Aware Of

BDSM is consensual. Always.

First and foremost, Consent is a HUGE factor in BDSM, and not going about it properly can really do some damage to you in ANY community. BDSM is based on the understanding that the parties involved are consenting adults and have explicitly communicated said consent.

In addition, the parties must adhere to the boundaries set within their relationship. While Dominants can be bossy, domineering, and powerful, if a submissive isn't into being spanked, then spankings are off the table. Likewise, if a Dominant does not want to have any form of genital contact during play, then it's the submissive's job to honour that boundary.

This is the difference between BDSM and sexual assault. A submissive who wants to be spanked in a scene is engaging in consensual BDSM play. A submissive that doesn't want to be spanked should not be spanked because that's a violent crime. People go to jail for that shit.

BDSM takes skill

Like any area in life, it takes time and practice to learn how to properly play with someone. For example, rope bondage is one of many BDSM activities that require a lot of knowledge and reading before acting out. There is a wide range of safety concerns that need to be kept in mind to properly do rope bondage. For those who have very little experience with rope bondage, rope can cut off circulation if done improperly, which can lead to nerve damage in serious cases. Sloppy ties can lead to a higher chance of the bottom getting hurt.

Rope bondage isn't the only thing that budding Dominants and submissives have to learn. They have to prepare for emergencies as well, like if a submissive enters subspace and withdraws too far into themselves to communicate, or a Dominant feels overwhelmed by a scene and needs to stop, for example.

If it takes more than a few play sessions for things to really click between you and your partner, that's pretty normal. Just remember to do a ton of research before jumping in, find a mentor if need be, and never try anything new without studying it, practising it, and creating a backup plan if something goes wrong.

BDSM isn't code for physical violence

Speaking of violent crimes, there's a huge difference between sadism/masochism and uninvited physical abuse. Physical abuse is an action that is both unwanted and non-consensual.

In a healthy BDSM relationship, it's the goal of both partners to please the other. The submissive sets boundaries and has a large amount of control over what happens in the relationship in regards to themselves.

It's important to remember that BDSM isn't just about tying a person up and calling it a day. The relationship is built on fulfilling your partner's needs, providing them pleasure, and constantly communicating to ensure you're doing both well. It's yet another reason why aftercare is so critical—not only because it's imperative that both partners feel safe and cared for, but because both must have a deep understanding of the other's boundaries, comfort levels, and sexual interests.

I've found that when a lot of newbies first hear of BDSM, they associate it with 'being mean', aggressive behaviour, and general sadism in a lot of cases. This couldn't be further from the truth. What typically gets lost in translation is the effort, understanding, and responsibility that comes with being a Dominant, or the control and vulnerability that comes with being a submissive. BDSM can be a sweet, fulfilling, and creative part of someone's life.

BDSM is NOT about sex

Well, not totally anyway. If you choose to dip into in any form of BDSM, it's more likely than not that you're looking for a release of the most unusual or hidden parts of you, an expression of complete and utter love, trust, and respect, or something completely new altogether. But there is nothing in particular you HAVE to get out of BDSM, but this lifestyle is about more than sex.

While a significant part of it to a lot of couples, BDSM goes way beyond sex, and a BDSM relationship (or any other type of relationship, for that matter) in any form should be far more than just about shagging someone. A D/s relationship totally comprised of sex isn't ever going to be a lasting one, and if you're looking for something deeper in your relationship with a potential partner, those relationships will feel completely one-sided.

Saying this, your relationships can of course be 100% sexual, but those are just fuck buddies in my opinion. However, BDSM is whatever you make of it, with people doing it for a variety of different reasons. People that feel this lifestyle is totally about sex, getting off, or anything the like, are totally missing the point.

Predators exist. Be aware, and be careful.

This lifestyle is not a place to practice domestic abuse or violence. Even still, you might find some predators lurking about. This can be at a munch, or on any dating service. They purposefully try to use the lifestyle to find someone to abuse because they've the increasingly stupid idea that anyone who claims submission is some sort of pushover.

They tend to target newer submissives because, in most cases, it's easier to manipulate them. Be aware that these people exist, and build a solid knowledge base about this lifestyle and how it pertains to you to better protect yourself from these people.

◇◇◇

Getting Started in BDSM

When done right, BDSM can be an incredibly fulfilling and intimate experience. Before you get started, remember that everyone has a different experience with and different opinions of BDSM and kink in general. There are a lot of truths, standards, and ways to otherwise navigate this lifestyle, which can definitely be intimidating to newbies. So here are a few things to help you get started on your journey into this lifestyle.

Think about what you want

This is high on my list of importance, so you should definitely pay attention. If you want to get into the world of BDSM, then you need to give some serious thought about what you want from this lifestyle before diving into it. It's important that you have a solid grasp on who you are, what you want, and what you need in terms of power exchange and kink. These things can all be tricky when first starting out. I recommend that those new to BDSM spend some time exploring themselves before seeking partners, whether simply play partners or otherwise.

This is something I typically have my partners do. I'll have them make a list with three categories: 'Yes', 'No', and 'Maybe'. I then have them write all the kinks, roleplays, positions, sexual experiences, and anything else they can think of under these categories. I've found this to be a great way to understand what they want in a relationship with me. You might want to give it a go.

Now take a look at your list, and think about what kind of role you want to take on during BDSM. If you like being in control or inflicting pain (and pleasure), you might just be a top. On the other hand, if you want to receive all of that humiliating control from a powerful presence, you may be a bottom. And if you want a little bit of both, then you're a switch. That means you get to play with different roles depending on your partner (or the scene at hand). Some play partners even switch up their Dominant and submissive roles, allowing the Dominant to occasionally become a submissive and vice versa.

BDSM is pretty flexible, but it's important to do a bit of soul searching and figure out what role you want to try out before hopping in. It's never fun to be topping mid-scene and realise that you actually want to bottom.

◇◇◇

When you want more than just a play partner

So you want more than to simply find someone to play with? I'm sure you know this, but finding a partner is hard enough in the vanilla world, but can seem damn-near impossible in the BDSM world.

Finding a kinky partner is a lot different from finding a vanilla one, mainly because most of the people you'd likely meet as potential partners would be all but eliminated. You want to find a quality partner, someone who meets your unique needs, but finding the best way to go about this can be difficult because most of the information out there pretty much only targets vanilla relationships.

Because I totally understand your plight, I'm going to take a moment to help you get sorted. And these things can of course be applied to whatever dynamic you're wanting to have.

So many lists, so little time

My first suggestion is to sit down and make a list of what you do and don't want in your relationships. When making these lists, you should take expectations like time spent with your partner, sexual encounters, and power exchange into consideration.

Here are some things you might want to think on about your kinky self:

- What are the types of kink activities I like?
- What kinks are important for my partner to share an interest?
- Which kink activities do I need, if any?
- What kink activities am I not open to at all?
- My thoughts on time:
- How often would I like to see my partner?
- How often should I hear from them?
- How much time together is too much for me?
- What are non-kink things I'd like to do with my partner?
- Does their work/life schedule balance with mine?
- My feelings about sex:
- Is having sex something I want to do?
- How long ago should my partner have been tested?
- What types of sexual activities am I interested in?
- What sexual activities are a no-go?
- How much sex do I need to be happy?

- How much am I willing to have?
- My feelings about power exchange:
- Is power exchange something I'm open to?
- Is power exchange something I need?
- Is it something I only want in the bedroom, or do I want a 24/7 relationship?
- How much control am I willing to give up?

These are all of course examples, but I think these questions are good starting points to ponder. And if you don't have all the answers to your questions, don't worry. Answer the questions you can, but give serious thought to those you can't answer. Then get out and start meeting people. But make sure you communicate the things you're unsure of to your potential partners. This will help to avoid any false expectations on either side, which can—and typically will—lead to hurt feelings later.

Once you have a basic understanding of what you want in your relationship, the next thing you need to consider is what you're offering in return in your relationship. This is something I absolutely can't stress the importance of enough. This is where fairness comes into play, which I'll get into in a moment.

One of the great things about BDSM is that agreements don't have to be the same. However, fairness is important, just as with any relationship. The more unfair—or better said, more unbalanced—the relationship is you're looking for, the more difficult it will be to find a partner, or become rather problematic if you're already in a relationship. While I do believe that in D/s dynamics the balance is more the submissive giving to the Dominant—as the balance in D/s dynamics lies in its imbalance. Now this is not to say the Dominant isn't supposed to give anything in return. That would make them a bit useless, to be honest, as they're bringing nothing but sex toys and a throbbing cock to the relationship.

At this point, you might be asking yourself how to break down what you're looking for versus what you're offering in a relationship, and do you do it in a way that's easy to communicate to a potential partner? Well, I'm glad you asked. First of all, it's important to realise that people aren't items we can customise to our specifications. No partner will meet every one of your needs and desires. It's pretty easy to write a huge list of specifications that a potential partner has to meet before you consider dating them, or drawing a line down the middle of a piece of paper, writing your wants on one side and what you're offering on the other. If you haven't noticed by now, I'm a fan of list-making. I tend to think better on paper.

As a matter of fact, go on and do this. I'll wait...

Now, take a look at your list from the viewpoint of a potential partner. Are the wants vs offering columns severely out of whack? Would you be interested in the arrangement you're offering if you were on the other side? If not, then it's likely that the arrangement you're looking for is one-sided, which is a great way to become lonely, horny, and frustrated. You should give some serious thought to whether you can make your expectations more balanced without compromising your needs before moving on.

Look, waiting around for the perfect partner can lead to missed opportunities to be in a relationship or relationships that you might be happy with. However, it's essential that you assess the things that are important to you in your relationships. What qualities do you need in a partner? Which are some that are simply nice to have? I'm not saying that you should compromise your needs or morals. However, if you seriously want to find a partner, you're probably going to have to compromise on some of your wants or expectations.

Find a Mentor

A lot of people nowadays would say that you don't need a mentor in BDSM. Technically speaking, this is true, as no one needs anything in BDSM other than consent, communication, and trust.

Now, I personally believe that newcomers to BDSM do need a mentor, as mentoring is a good way for them—especially submissives—to learn about this lifestyle. People will say that if you want information about BDSM, Google is only a click away, which is true if you're looking for nothing more than basic information. However, a website can only do so much, as it can only tell you how to navigate certain areas of this lifestyle or give insight as to what to look out for. At some point, a newbie is going to have to talk to someone.

There are a lot of benefits to having a mentor, which include:

- Having a trusted source to turn to with questions.
- Learning how to navigate the world of dungeons, play parties, and scenes.
- Guidance amidst an online world of misinformation
- A second opinion, if you begin to wonder if you're on the right track.
- Ideas for how to go about doing this BDSM thing.

Being involved with BDSM is something that is so completely different from vanilla life, that newbies are often overwhelmed with what they see. Furthermore, since there are so many predators who prey upon the vulnerability and ignorance of new submissives, it's helpful to have an experienced individual act as a protector and to help guide a new submissive through the early stages of this lifestyle. Of course, this pertains more to submissives rather than Dominants, but the concept of a mentor is helpful to both.

Here are a couple of things that are important when approaching or being approached by a possible mentor.

Mentors should be experienced

As I mentioned, a mentor should be an experienced individual. That is the first thing that should be sought out. I am amazed at how many submissives decide to choose a mentor who has only a few months or a year of experience in this lifestyle. That person is NOT a mentor, instead being a person with limited knowledge who is most likely preying upon the submissive, using the submissive to practise their supposed dominance.

A mentor is there to pass along knowledge gained by their being part of our lifestyle for a number of years—possibly decades. Thus, it is crucial for anyone calling themselves a mentor be someone who has been part of this lifestyle for a significant amount of time, and has been a practitioner for a large part of it. Getting references would do you well here.

Mentors should be trustworthy

The second thing that a mentor must be is trustworthy. Here is where the situation can enter a grey area very quickly. It is common for a new submissive to fall for their mentor. This is a person who is going to act in a manner that resembles a Dominant; however, you've to understand that they are not that person. The line between owning someone and being a mentor is clear. There is a degree of trust that is handed over to a mentor in the same way a therapist or counsellor is given trust. For them to betray that trust by personally involving themselves moves into the area of deceit.

This means that the mentor needs to understand the limits of their relationship with the submissive completely. One who crosses the line is the lowest form of scum there is. I have more respect for someone who is upfront and obvious about their intentions, especially if they equally find themselves falling for the person they're mentoring. Anyone with any intelligence can pick them up instantly. Predatory mentors are a bit more difficult to figure out, especially if they've been at it a while. You definitely need to be wary of these people. I talk a bit more about predators in Chapter 6.

With all of this said, I think mentors are awesome, and I also think anyone new to BDSM should consider finding a mentor before rushing headfirst into a relationship. When you connect with the right person, a mentor can be an excellent sounding board and support for you as you learn and grow, and could be a way to prevent you from making many of the mistakes that are commonplace today.

◇◇◇

Finding Play Partners

One of the most difficult things about BDSM is finding people to play around with. Sex is already taboo in the United States—let alone BDSM. However, there are a few options that might be immediately available to you to find Dominants, submissives, and other kinky people to play with.

For one, if you're currently in a relationship, talk to your partner about BDSM. They may have experiences of their own with kink, or they may be interested in experimenting with Dominant and submissive roles. Plus, a romantic or sexual partner is a great tagalong for any local workshops and events, and having your significant other by your side at parties can help calm a beginner's nerves.

I talk a bit more about finding play partners and other kinky peeps in Chapter 6.

Practise, Practise, Practise

This ties back into what I said earlier about BDSM taking skill. It takes loads of research and fine-tuning. Whether it's tying that perfect knot, slapping a submissive at just the right speed and position, or figuring out your favourite position to be dominated, improving as a top or bottom is all about studying and working for it. And when it comes to more risky play that means spending plenty of time planning beforehand.

If you want to learn the basics of BDSM play, you might want to try finding a workshop in your local area or seeking out a proper mentor.

◇◇◇

BDSM vs. Abuse

If you feel threatened in a bad way, if your submission is forced or something about the relationship makes you think or feel bad all the time, and you get no comfort from it, it's more likely abuse than a BDSM relationship.

I've listed a few differences between the two that I think you should be aware of:

- BDSM is about the mutual respect demonstrated between two open-minded people. Abuse is about the lack of respect that one person demonstrates to another person.

- BDSM is about loving each other completely and without reservation in an alternative way. Abuse is hurtful, and very damaging both emotionally and spiritually to the submissive.

- BDSM is about the building of a trusting relationship between two consenting adult partners. Abuse is about the breach of trust between an authority figure and the person in their care.

- BDSM is about a shared enjoyment of controlled erotic pain and/or humiliation for mutual pleasure. Abuse is a form of out-of-control physical violence and/or personal or emotional degradation of the submissive.

- BDSM frees a submissive from the restraints of years of vanilla conditioning to explore a buried part of themselves. Abuse binds a submissive to a lonely and solitary life of shame, fear and secrecy—imprisoning the very core of their being.

- BDSM builds self-esteem as a person discovers and embraces a long-hidden part of themselves. Abuse shatters and destroys a person's self-esteem, leaving a tattered path of self-hatred in its wake.

Warning Signs

A classic warning sign that a BDSM relationship is not healthy is when one of the partners tells the other not to talk about it with anyone else, or not to participate in the community. Now of course, a basic respect for each other and your relationship should be maintained, as going into intimate details, airing your dirty laundry for the masses, or trashing your partner loudly at a play party is just not classy. But having one or two trusted friends to turn to in times of trouble can be essential to a submissive, and a wise Dominant would encourage a submissive to seek out viable support rather than discourage it.

Chapter 2:

HISTORIC ORIGINS OF BDSM

The historical origins of BDSM are obscure, at best. Especially since a lot of earlier depictions of BDSM activity have been lost to history. But there are a few things that I do know, and will do my best to shed some light on them for you. So let's get started, okay?

◇◇◇

From Beatings to Bettie Page

One of the oldest proven depictions of sadomasochistic activity was found in an Etruscan tomb called the *Tomba della Fustigazione* (flogging tomb) in the *Necropolis of Monterozzi* near Tarquinia, Italy. Dated approximately 490 BC, the tomb is named after a fresco (painting) of two men portrayed beating a woman with a cane and a hand during an erotic situation was found inside the tomb.

Other depictions of BDSM activity can typically be found in religion. For instance, during the third century CE, a Greek religious group called the Cult of Orthia gave rise to the *diamastigosis*—the best-known of Spartan rituals.

This annual practice took place in the *Sanctuary of Artemis Orthia*, one of the most important religious areas of ancient Sparta, and involved the flogging of the Ephebos, or teenagers. The diamastigosis was used as both a religious ritual and a test of the boys' bravery and resistance to pain.

Another reference related to flogging is to be found in *Juvenal and Persius*, the sixth book of the *Satires of Juvenal*, written in the late first and early second centuries CE by ancient Roman poet Decimus Junius Juvenalis. Other mentions can be found in Satyricon, written in the late first century AD by Gaius Petronius Arbiter. The book has several mentions of slaves being whipped for sexual arousal.

Beyond the Mediterranean, other ancient civilisations also left traces of what we might now call BDSM-related activity. Ancient Egyptian temple reliefs occasionally depict bound captives in highly stylised, almost sensual postures, while some Nubian and Ethiopian artworks suggest ceremonial binding. In Japan, the martial art of hojojutsu (rope restraint) was eventually eroticised into shibari and kinbaku during the Edo period, becoming an intricate form of visual and sensual expression. In medieval Arabic erotic literature, such as *The Perfumed Garden*, playful slapping, pinching, and biting are recorded as part of lovemaking.

Other stories date as far back as the third and fourth centuries involving humans who have had themselves voluntarily bound, flogged or whipped as a substitute for sex or as part of foreplay.

The Kama Sutra is considered by many to be one of the first written resources dealing with sadomasochistic activities and safety rules. It describes four different kinds of hitting during lovemaking, the allowed regions of the human body to target and different kinds of joyful 'cries of pain' practised. It clearly highlights in historic texts that impact play, biting, and pinching during sexual activities should only be performed consensually, since only some women consider these actions to be joyful.

Moving forward into the medieval and Renaissance periods, flagellation took on both sacred and profane roles. Some Christian penitents whipped themselves as a form of religious devotion, and in certain cases, the practice drifted into erotic territory. Early modern brothel records and risqué woodcuts from the 16th and 17th centuries show that erotic whipping, binding, and role-play were already established amusements for paying clients long before the 18th century.

Texts with sadomasochistic connotation began appearing worldwide on a regular basis during the following centuries. There are reports of people willingly being bound or whipped during the fourteenth century, as a form of foreplay or substitute for sex. Other sources claim that BDSM is a distinct form of sexual behaviour originating at the beginning of the eighteenth century, with the Marquis de Sade and Leopold von Sacher-Masoch being associated with the terms sadism and masochism, respectively.

However, John Cleland's 1749 novel *Fanny Hill* mentions a flogging scene. There are also reports of the sexual games played in brothels, which included their specialising in flagellation as early as 1769. Neither Sade nor Sacher-Masoch became known until after the late 1700s.

BDSM ideas and imagery have existed on the borders of Western culture throughout the twentieth century. Robert V. Bienvenu studied the origins of fetishism and sadomasochism and, in 1998, published his findings, called *The Development of Sadomasochism as a Cultural Style in the United States*. In his report, he attributed the origins of modern-day BDSM to three sources: European Fetish (1928), American Fetish (1934), and Gay Leather (1950).

Irving Klaw produced some of the first commercial BDSM-themed films and photography during the 1950s and 1960s, and published comics by iconic bondage artists John Willie and Eric Stanton— most notably with model Bettie Page. Page became one of the first successful models in the area of fetish photography and is easily one of the most famous pin-up girls of American mainstream culture.

Italian author and designer Guido Crepax was deeply influenced by Stanton's work, creating the style and development of European adult comics. Photographers Helmut Newton and Robert Mapplethorpe are well-known examples of using BDSM-related themes in modern photography, and their work still influences others to this day—myself included.

During the latter half of the 20th century, John Norman's *Gor* novels—beginning with *Tarnsman of Gor* in 1966—introduced a fictional world in which hierarchical power dynamics, consensual slavery, and ritualised dominance were central themes. While controversial, the series influenced some BDSM communities by providing a framework for exploring consensual dominance and submission in imaginative, narrative-driven contexts. Readers were inspired to experiment with power exchange and ritualised roles in their own relationships, often citing the Gor series as a point of reference alongside more visual or experiential media like bondage photography or fetish art.

Throughout all of these eras, one thing has remained constant: communities built around BDSM have often needed to communicate under the radar. For centuries, this was done through whispered introductions, personal referrals, and discreet tokens or signals. In the modern era, that desire for subtle identification eventually took physical form in a symbol—the BDSM emblem.

◇◇◇

The BDSMblem

Now, if you've started doing any sort of research into BDSM, I'm sure you've seen the BDSMblem at some point, because it's damn near everywhere. From jewellery to mouse pads, the BDSMblem has become a huge part of this lifestyle. The interesting thing I've found is that a lot of people think that it's a lot older a symbol than

Fig. 1.1.: The emblem described in
'The Story of O'

it really is. But this is likely because the BDSMblem is based on much older and well-known symbols. If you've ever wondered about where the BDSMblem came from, then allow me to enlighten you.

Around 1995, a discussion on AOL (because... the 90's) set the course for what we now know as the BDSMblem (originally written as 'BDSM Emblem', but was later changed). Anyway, there was a general idea among the group members that a symbol was needed to represent this lifestyle. They decided that the symbol needed to be a bit mysterious, so when worn, it wouldn't attract a lot of attention from 'vanilla observers'. It did, however, need to be easily recognised by those who knew what it was.

Steve Quagmyr, one of the discussion leaders, created an emblem reminiscent of the Yin-Yang design. The choice of design was influenced by a description of the ring that 'O' was given in Pauline Réage's 1954 novel 'The Story of O'. The ring as described in the book, 'bore a three-spoked wheel ... with each spoke spiralling back upon itself ...'

Quagmyr described the metallic colour as a representation of the chains or irons of BDSM and the black background as a celebration of the controlled dark side of BDSM sexuality. The curved lines symbolise the 'lash as it swings', and the circle shape represents the unity and oneness of a 'community that protects its own.'

After a while, people started spreading the BDSMblem across the internet without properly understanding the background information of it. A lot of people seem to consider any Triskele as a BDSM symbol. The BDSM Emblem was created to allow lifestylers a way to identify themselves to each other secretly.

The Design of the BDSMblem

Quagmyr's idea behind the BDSMblem was initially proposed and promoted in a specific manner. It was to be a symbol based on the Triskelion, and it was supposed to enable those who wanted to find others of like interests to identify themselves to each other in a way that wouldn't out themselves to a potentially persecuting public. For that reason, the symbol was based on one that would pretty much go unnoticed.

While the Triskelion is the basic shape of the Emblem, not all Triskeles are BDSMblems, despite what a LOT of people have been led to believe. The Triskelion that the BDSMblem is based upon is an ancient shape that has had varied uses and meanings in many cultures, including the Japanese Mitsudomoe, Korean Sam Taegeuk, and Tibetan Dharmacakra (also known as Gankyil).

It's the details of the design that make the BDSMblem what it is. As I mentioned, the BDSMblem was created to look common enough to go unnoticed. To aid in identification, it was created with very specific and meaningful details. Those details are the three black inner fields, which represent a celebration of the controlled dark side of BDSM sexuality, the metal and metallic colour—typically

Fig. 1.2: BDSMblem

silver or gold—of the medallion (the outer line), representing the chains or irons of BDSM servitude/ownership, and holes through the inner fields.

The holes represent the 'incompleteness of any individual within the BDSM context', because BDSM cannot be done alone, because no matter how 'together' and 'whole' individuals may be, there remains a void within them that can only be filled by a complementary other. D-types need s-types, and s-types need D-types. There's no getting around this very basic fact, no matter what anyone may try and lead you to believe.

The resemblance to a Yin-Yang symbol was actually done on purpose by Quagmyr. The curved outline of Yin and Yang represents the border between where one ends and the other begins, the curved borders on the BDSMblem represent the three divisions of BDSM: Bondage/Discipline, Dominance/Submission, and Sadism/Masochism. Secondly, the three-way creed of BDSM behaviour: Safe, Sane, and Consensual. Thirdly, the three divisions of the BDSM community: Tops, Bottoms, and Switches.

The Meaning of the BDSMblem

The BDSMblem has no 'obvious' symbolism because it was created to be enigmatic. To the vanilla observers who would be put off by BDSM, it's merely an attractive piece of jewellery. Thus, we can wear it freely as a salute, or nod, to other lifestylers if we should happen to cross each other's paths in our daily lives.

◇◇◇

At-a-Glance: A Very Brief Timeline of BDSM History

c. 490 BC – *Tomba della Fustigazione*, Etruscan fresco showing erotic flogging.

3rd century CE – Spartan diamastigosis ritual flogging in the *Cult of Orthia*.

Late 1st–early 2nd century CE – Roman literature (*Satires of Juvenal, Satyricon of Petronius*) depicts slaves whipped for sexual arousal.

3rd–5th century CE – *Kama Sutra* describes consensual hitting, biting, pinching, and cries of pain in lovemaking.

Ancient Egypt – Temple reliefs and art depict bound figures in sensual or ceremonial contexts.

Medieval Arabic world – Erotic texts like *The Perfumed Garden* record playful pain in foreplay.

Edo-period Japan (1603–1868) – Rope bondage evolves from martial *hojojutsu* into erotic *shibari/kinbaku*.

14th–17th centuries – Reports of consensual whipping and binding in Europe; religious flagellation sometimes blurs into eroticism; early brothels offer 'discipline' services.

1749 – *Fanny Hill* includes a flogging scene; brothels specialising in flagellation active by 1769.

Late 1700s – Lives and writings of Marquis de Sade and Leopold von Sacher-Masoch later give us 'sadism' and 'masochism.'

1928–1950 – Foundations of modern BDSM culture identified: European Fetish, American Fetish, and Gay Leather communities.

1950s–60s – Irving Klaw, Bettie Page, John Willie, Eric Stanton popularise bondage imagery.

1966–present – John Norman's *Gor* novels depict male-dominant/female-submissive worlds, influencing popular imagination around power exchange dynamics in fantasy.

1954 – *The Story of O* by Pauline Réage is published, becoming one of the most influential BDSM-themed novels of the 20th century.

Mid–late 20th century – Photographers Helmut Newton and Robert Mapplethorpe bring BDSM themes into fine art.

1995 – Steve Quagmyr designs the BDSM emblem (*BDSMblem*), blending Triskelion, Story of O, and Yin-Yang influences.

Chapter 3:

COMMON BDSM TERMS

I've already used a few terms that are commonplace in BDSM. But there are a lot of other terms that you're likely going to notice when speaking with others in the lifestyle, or reading about BDSM, or hear in virtually every BDSM or kink-related event.

I'm going to cover some of these terms and their definitions, now you've a better understanding of what BDSM is.

◇◇◇

24/7
A dynamic in which partners engage in BDSM full-time—twenty-four hours a day, seven days a week.

Aftercare
The activities that take place after a scene, during which partners spend time together to transition back to everyday life. This can range from a few minutes of cuddling to extended holding and reassurance. It is the Dominant's responsibility to help the sub-

missive calm down, feel cared for, checked on, and emotionally stable.

Age Play
Play in which one person assumes an adult role while another takes on a child role.

Animal Play
Play in which one partner—usually the submissive—portrays an animal. The most common subcategories are Kitty Play, Pony Play, and Puppy Play. Synonymous with Pet Play.

BDSM
An umbrella term describing bondage, discipline, dominance and submission, and sadomasochism. It encompasses a wide range of sexual and lifestyle practices involving consensual power exchange, impact play, restraint, and roleplay.

Blood Play
An erotic or sexual activity in which participants extract blood from their partners, using tools such as razor blades, knives, needles, or biting. Blood play often intersects with a blood fetish or other forms of edgeplay. Some individuals find the sight, taste, or pain of blood erotic. Blood play can be extremely dangerous or deadly and is not recommended for novices.

Bottom
A subclass of submissive who temporarily gives up control in a scene to receive emotional or sexual satisfaction from their submission to a Top. A bottom's degree of submission varies according to desire and negotiated agreements, and power exchanges can occur to differing degrees.

Bottom Drop
A brief period of emotional low or depression experienced by a bottom after an intense scene. Also called sub-drop or submissive rebound.

Breath Play
BDSM play involving the restriction of oxygen to heighten sexual arousal and intensify orgasm. Methods include strangulation, suffocation, or smothering. When performed on oneself, it is called auto-erotic asphyxiation. Breath play is extremely dangerous or potentially fatal and is not recommended for novices.

Command
A clear directive given by a Dominant that is expected to be obeyed without hesitation. Commands may be spoken, written, or conveyed through established signals.

Consent
Mutual agreement to the terms of a scene or an ongoing BDSM relationship.

Consensual Non-Consensuality (CNC)
A style of BDSM play in which participants agree to behave as if the activity is non-consensual, while all parties are aware and have given consent.

Contract
A written or verbal agreement outlining expectations, limits, and responsibilities within a power exchange or BDSM relationship, commonly used for 24/7 dynamics. Contracts should not be created during initial encounters.

Daddy / Daddy Dominant
A partner who assumes a fatherly role within a relationship, of-

ten—but not always—acting as the Dominant.

Dominant/Dom/Domme/Dominatrix

These titles refer to the person in charge or the one who exercises control in a D/s relationship—the person who is obeyed. They can be used for either male or female Dominants. 'Dom' is short for Dominant, while both Domme and Dominatrix refer to female Dominants.

Some argue that a Domme is simply a female Dominant, and that Dominatrix applies only to those who charge for services—but that's incorrect. Only professional Dommes charge for their services.

DM

Dungeon Monitor/Master—a person who volunteers to supervise the interactions between participants at a play party to ensure their safety.

D/s (Domination/submission)

A type of BDSM dynamic in which one partner (the Dominant) exercises control over another (the submissive) with the submissive's consent. D/s can range from scenes that last only minutes to full-time 24/7 relationships. Agreements, rituals, and protocols often guide behaviour and power exchange.

Dungeon

A room or area equipped for BDSM activities. Often called a playroom, a dungeon may contain bondage furniture, restraints, and other equipment.

Dynamic

Any BDSM relationship or arrangement between participants, regardless of its style, duration, or intensity. A dynamic may be casual, scene-based, or a long-term 24/7 arrangement.

Edge play
BDSM play that carries a risk of physical or emotional harm. The definition of edge play is subjective and varies between participants, so there is no universal list of activities that qualify. Certain practices, however, are commonly considered edge play, including fire play, gun play, rough body play, breath play, and blood play. Edge play is also sometimes used to describe erotic sexual denial.

Fetish
A sexual desire in which gratification is strongly linked to a specific object, body part, activity, or experience. Fetishes may or may not involve BDSM practices.

Fem-Domme
A female Dominant who takes the leading role in a BDSM dynamic or scene.

Fin-Domme
A female Dominant who primarily receives financial tribute or gifts from submissives (sometimes called 'paypigs') in exchange for attention, control, or humiliation. Financial domination (findom) may or may not include physical scenes.

Fuckboy
A male or female, respectively, who engages in sexual activity without intention of dating, committing, or pursuing emotional connection.

Funishment
A portmanteau of 'fun' and 'punishment', funishment is a specific type of punishment used in a BDSM relationship to spark an erotic encounter. Unlike traditional BDSM punishments,

funishments arise from trivial misdeeds rather than serious behavioural infractions. While pain may be involved, it is typically mild or playful.

Funishment is also called play punishment.

Gorean/Gor
A BDSM lifestyle inspired by John Norman's Gor series of fiction novels. Relationships are typically Master/slave, and participants may adopt the culture, rituals, and protocols depicted in the books.

Gun Play
BDSM play that involves a loaded or unloaded firearm. Guns can be used as props or penetrative objects. Gun play is considered extreme edge play, typically practiced under RACK or PRICK principles rather than SSC.

Hard Limit
An activity that must not be done in a scene or relationship. Violating a hard limit is generally considered just cause for ending the scene or, in some cases, the relationship.

Kajira
The term for a female slave, or 'slave-girl,' in John Norman's Gor novels. Duties may include sexual servitude as well as household management, artistic skills, wearing an appealing outfit, and addressing the Master in a specific manner. Male slaves are called kajirus.

Kinbaku
A Japanese word which means 'tight binding', and is a type of rope bondage which involves tying up the bottom using simple yet visually intricate patterns, usually with several pieces of thin rope.

Sometimes used interchangeably with Shibari, although some suggest that Kinbaku describes the sexual experience as a whole, while Shibari refers specifically to the aesthetic rope bondage.

Kinky
BDSM activities or individuals with an SM orientation.

Kitty Play
Play in which the submissive takes the role of being a feline.

Leather/Leathermen
Terms frequently used by the gay male community to describe behaviours that typically include SM activities. Also referred to as 'Leathersex'.

Limits
Activities that participants in a play scene or dynamic feel strongly about, usually referring to prohibited activities. Both Dominants and submissives can set limits.

Little
An individual who identifies as or role plays as a young child.

Master/Mistress
Titles for the Dominant or controlling partner in a Master/slave relationship, typically within a full-time D/s dynamic. This may describe a couple who live together and practise these roles 24/7, or two people who always assume their roles when together. The term can also refer to someone highly skilled in a particular discipline—for example, a Master of Ropework.

Mommy
Someone who takes on a mother role in a relationship and is often, but not always, a Dominatrix.

M/s (Master/slave)
A D/s relationship in which the submissive (slave) gives full consent to the Dominant (Master) to exercise authority over most aspects of their life. M/s dynamics often involve structured rules, rituals, and protocols, and may be part of 24/7 lifestyles.

Mummification
The practice of immobilising the body, typically by wrapping it in multiple layers of tight, thin plastic sheeting. Safety precautions—especially ensuring the face, mouth, and nose remain unobstructed—are essential. Mummification is often used to heighten the sensation of total physical helplessness and can be combined with other forms of sensation play.

Munch
A gathering of people into BDSM, held at a vanilla venue, usually a restaurant. Drinking alcohol is typically prohibited.

Negotiation
The consensual agreements between Top and bottom, either spoken or written as a contract, outlining hard limits, preferences, punishments, and expected behaviours. Negotiation always occurs outside of roles and before any play begins.

Newbie
Someone new to BDSM.

Owners
Individuals who have possession of another, usually a slave or pet.

Paypig
A submissive, usually male, who gives money, gifts, or financial control to a Dominant, typically a Fin-Domme, as part of a financial domination (findom) dynamic.

Pet Play
A form of play in which one partner—usually the submissive—portrays an animal. The most common subcategories are Kitty Play, Pony Play, and Puppy Play. Synonymous with Animal Play.

Play Party
A BDSM event in which many people engage in Scenes.

Polyamory
The practice, desire, or acceptance of having an intimate and/or sexual relationship involving more than two individuals at a time, with the knowledge and consent of everyone involved.

Polyfidelity
A form of polyamory in which all members are considered equal partners and agree to be sexually active only with other members of the group. The term originated with Kerista Village, a San Francisco commune that practised polyfidelity around 1971. Also called polyexclusivity.

Power Exchange
An alternative term for SM or BDSM, denoting the consensual giving and taking of power, along with the mutual responsibilities of care and trust that come with the exchange.

PRICK
Personal Responsibility, Informed Consensual Kink, a term that began circulating around 2009. It is a variation of Risk-Aware Consensual Kink (RACK).

This philosophy, observed within parts of the BDSM community, emphasises that participants engaging in risky sexual behaviours are personally responsible and must give informed consent after fully understanding and considering the risks involved.

Protocol(s)
Written or unwritten rules and guidelines followed by BDSM participants. Most commonly used in strict 24/7 relationships.

Pro-Domme
A professional Dominatrix who is paid for services. While many assume the term Dominatrix always refers to a paid professional, it is often used less frequently within non-professional BDSM communities.

Pony Play
Pet play in which the submissive takes the role of a horse.

Punishment
A disciplinary act administered when a submissive or slave has purposely been disobedient and has knowingly disobeyed a command or done something incorrectly, brought on by an act of defiance.

Puppy Play
Pet play in which the submissive takes the role of being a canine.

RACK
Used by some to describe a philosophy that is generally permissive of certain risky sexual behaviours, provided the participants are fully aware of the risks involved.

RACK places the responsibility squarely on the shoulders of those engaging in BDSM play: they must understand the risks of the activities they choose and ensure that all play is fully consensual.

Rough Body Play
A form of impact play in which participants strike each other

without the use of toys, often by punching, slapping, kicking, or otherwise being physically rough.

Safeword
A pre-agreed phrase that stops a scene when used. When a participant utters a safeword, all activity halts—either entirely or to allow renegotiation of the scene. Commonly, the colours of traffic signals are used: red to stop, yellow to slow or modify, and green to indicate that all is well.

Scene
A defined period of time during which a Dominant or Top and a submissive or bottom engage in a BDSM session. Also called 'play' or 'work'. In contrast, 'the scene' refers to the broader BDSM lifestyle as a whole.

Shibari
From the Japanese verb shibaru, meaning 'to tie'. While it can apply to tying any object, it has become the universal term for Japanese-style rope bondage. Sometimes used interchangeably with Kinbaku, although Shibari often refers specifically to the aesthetic aspect of the rope work, while Kinbaku emphasises the sexual experience as a whole.

Sip
A gathering of people into BDSM, held at a vanilla venue such as a café, where only non-alcoholic drinks are served.

Slave
An individual who has consented to be wholly under the control of a Master or Dominant.

Slosh
A gathering of people into BDSM, held at a vanilla venue such as

a restaurant or pub. Drinking alcohol is allowed.

Soft Limit
Something that someone will do only in special circumstances or when highly aroused.

SSC
Safe, sane and consensual.

- **Safe**: attempts should be made to identify and prevent risks to health.
- **Sane**: activities should be undertaken in a sane and sensible state of mind.
- **Consensual**: all activities should involve the fully informed consent of all parties involved.

Sub-Drop
The term refers to the brief depression a submissive sometimes falls into after an intense scene. Also known as submissive rebound. Synonymous with bottom drop.

Submissive
An individual who gives up control and in return gets emotional or sexual satisfaction. Submissives want to be taken care of and to be given behavioural structure by a Dominant, which may include serving or being used by the Dominant.

Subspace
An altered mental state that a submissive can enter, usually during intense play sessions. Subspace is sometimes described as a form of hypnotic or trance-like state, which can be self-attained or facilitated by a Dominant. Attempting to reach subspace is not recommended for novices.

Swinger

A person who participates in the swinging lifestyle. Swingers can be of any sexual orientation and may be married couples or single individuals.

Swinging

The practice of exchanging sexual partners, often to increase the variety or frequency of sexual experiences.

Switch

A person who takes on both Dominant and submissive roles, typically with different partners, without identifying exclusively as either.

Taken in Hand

Male-led, 24/7 heterosexual relationships in which the man assumes control. The man's role is to make decisions and assign tasks, while the woman's role is to please and obey. These relationships may include BDSM dynamics, but do not necessarily require them.

Top

A subclass of a Dominant, this is the person in control during a scene or play, though they may not identify as a Dominant outside it. The term originated in the gay community, where the 'giver' performed the penetration and the 'bottom' received. It was later adopted by the wider BDSM community, including straight practitioners.

Topping from the Bottom

A situation in which the bottom in a scene attempts to control the Top, dictating what to do and how to do it. This behaviour can be considered bratty, particularly by some pro-Dommes.

Toys

Implements such as floggers, whips, canes, clamps, etc. Also known as 'tools'.

Unicorn

A bisexual single person, usually female, who is willing to have sex with or enter into a relationship with an established couple.

Vanilla

Refers to someone or something that is not kinky, or to behaviours outside the BDSM community. Also used to describe sexual activity that is generally considered conventional.

Wannabe

Someone who believes or claims they are knowledgeable about BDSM but lacks experience or understanding. Often seen among new Dominants, and can include predators pretending to be part of the community.

Chapter 4:

BDSM ROLES

N o matter how you found BDSM or decided to explore this lifestyle, one of the first questions some people have is about BDSM roles, and where they may fit—are they Dominant or submissive? Let's explore the various types of roles in BDSM to help you try and figure out where you might fall on the BDSM totem pole.

◇◇◇

Sorting Through the Labels

Roles are an important aspect of this lifestyle. And while I absolutely don't agree with most of the titles that have been creeping their way into this lifestyle—a few of which you'll read in a moment—everyone needs to identify themselves so other lifestylers will know if they might be compatible with each other.

Each person who has an interest in BDSM has their own opinion about what a Dominant or submissive is, and technically, they're all correct—for the people expressing them. Even if you don't agree with the majority of these opinions (which I don't), it's what it is for the time being.

◇◇◇

BDSM Roles: S-Types

First, I'll talk about the various s-type roles. Since FetLife has been ramping up in popularity over the years, there are a lot of new titles popping up, none of which existed when I started in this lifestyle. Titles like princess, warrior submissive, and a lot of others that I find utterly fucking ridiculous.

Because I will personally never acknowledge those as being a legitimate part of this lifestyle, I'll stick to the more common ones—submissives, slaves, littles, pets, and bottoms.

- **Submissives**: A submissive is someone who desires to give up control of themselves, or control of certain aspects of their lives, to a Dominant. There are a lot of different 'types' of submissive now—one ridiculous type after another. But moving on...

- **Slaves**: A slave is someone who consensually gives total control to their Master/Owner—often giving up much or all of their rights to limits, safewords, or negotiation. Gorean relationships and the titular character in Story of O are good examples of slave types.

- **Littles**: A little is someone who identifies as or role plays as a young child.

- **Pets**: Pets are bottoms who enjoy animal play, or a submissive or slave who is considered property like domestic animals. Pets will not necessarily have an animal persona—but it can happen.

- **Bottoms**: During play sessions, a bottom is the person who gives up control, or who receives physical sensation from a Top.

With all of this said, there is one prevailing fact that I want you to ALWAYS keep firmly in mind: Submission is something that must be EARNED in a D/s relationship. This includes yours—no matter what people may attempt to make you believe.

Are You Cut Out to Be a Submissive?

Believe it or not, not everyone is capable of being a submissive. It's even possible that you're not really cut out for it. We all have different thresholds for what we can and can't do, but realising you can't be submissive isn't the end of the world. So, how do you know if you can be a submissive or not?

I'm not going to cover bedroom submissives or kinky bottoms. The type of submissive I'm talking about here is a relationship submissive—someone who is subordinate in everyday things. A bedroom submissive or a kinky bottom is something entirely different. Anyone can be submissive for weekends or set amounts of time, or be a bottom for a short period of time. What I'm talking about is submission on a personality or character level. You're going to either agree or disagree with this, but you've already gotten this far, so you might as well keep reading, right?

People develop specific personality traits that then define whether they can be submissive or not. There are a few, however, that don't lend themselves to being a vital part of submission and can, in fact, cause a lot of friction in their relationship with their partners. If these can't be curbed, then it's likely you're not cut out to be a submissive.

Poor submissive personality traits include:
- Selfishness and Self-importance
- Domineering Behaviour
- Being Manipulative

• Being Bratty

On Selfishness and Self-importance

Selfishness and self-importance are synonymous in the case of damaging personality traits to have when you're trying to be submissive. Most new and/or untrained submissives tell themselves that they won't submit unless they get something in return.

For example, I once had a partner who was like this, and after a while, it got to the point that she wouldn't want to play unless she was getting an orgasm or something like that. She was being selfish and made her needs and desires more important than mine. Needless to say, I ended that relationship.

Now, before you start burning torches and storming my apartment, this isn't to say that I believe D/s dynamics shouldn't be at all about the submissive and all about the Dominant, but as I mentioned before, I do believe that in D/s dynamics, the balance is more about the submissive giving to the Dominant.

To continue, this went against what we had negotiated, and it appeared as though she was trying to somehow manipulate our dynamic, and her brattiness was increasing beyond what I chose to deal with. This also fell under our dynamic, becoming significantly one-sided, which I talked about back in Chapter 1 as being problematic in a relationship.

With this said, no matter what people may tell you, it's okay for a submissive to be selfish—but within negotiated parameters. A few 'selfish' things you can do for yourself include taking some alone time, spoiling yourself a bit, and learning to be firm about sticking with your limits—assuming they're actually limits. I'll give you a few examples of each:

Taking some alone time: Having a bit of 'me time' can help you re-focus on your place with your Dominant, and re-centre yourself from anything you may be going through. Because, as nice as it may seem to be with your partner all the bloody time, at some point you're going to need some room to breathe.

Spoiling yourself: Doing things like going out to eat, going to a movie, or having a quiet bubble bath are all good things, and there's absolutely nothing wrong with wanting to do these things. It might just be the mood booster you're needing.

Sticking to your limits: You'll find Dominants who will tell you that submissives or slaves don't have, or can't have, limits. This is totally not true—especially if you've negotiated these things. You have limits set in place for a reason—because those are the things you're not comfortable doing, and shouldn't be made to do until YOU are ready. Watch out for blokes who employ coercion as a tactic to stop you exercising your limits. Limits can be pushed—but shouldn't blatantly be broken.

However, if you're setting limits for things that wouldn't be seen as a limit—like wearing a collar, or being subjected to orgasm denial—you're just being manipulative, and should re-examine your thoughts on submission, and whether you might actually be one or not. I'll talk more about being manipulative in a bit.

Whatever you choose to do with yourself, keep in mind that there is a proper way to go about doing this, because, as I mentioned, it's okay within certain parameters, and should be a totally acceptable request to your partner. However, there is still a respect that is or should be expected of you, so don't take the things I said as a way to be insubordinate. Be sure you communicate and negotiate these times, and how you'd like to exercise them with your partner, and have fun.

On Domineering Behaviour

As far as domineering behaviour is concerned, I know—just like every other Dominant should know—that no submissive is perfect. There are some days you're just not going to want to do something requested of you. However, if you're constantly fighting for control in your dynamic, then you're not truly submitting or lending yourself completely to your submission, which can and will become problematic in the relationship with your Dominant.

Some people out there—typically those new to this lifestyle—seem to claim the title of 'alpha submissive' as a way to assert they don't really want to give up control of themselves to a Dominant.

What is an alpha submissive, you ask? Alpha submissives are typically found in BDSM houses or leather families. They are the 'head submissive' or the submissive with the most seniority and experience. In the case of polyamorous relationships, an alpha submissive is the term used for the most powerful submissive, with the term only being used in a polyamorous relationship where more than one submissive is involved.

When people refer to themselves as an alpha submissive, they're typically not saying it to mean they're the first submissive or the submissive with the most responsibility in a group. They're usually saying it for various reasons, most of which stem from somehow misunderstanding the term, or as a protective measure from a damaging relationship. They can also be saying it to hide some sort of insecurity, or because of feminist ideologies that reject traditional submission, or because of cultural narratives that view any form of surrender as weakness—a sadly growing view in today's society.

Almost any experienced person in this lifestyle would agree with me in saying that new people declaring themselves an alpha submissive is a red flag. In most cases, it indicates that the person isn't fully comfortable with their submission, and very likely not ready for a D/s relationship.

With this said, being a submissive means that you have chosen to follow a Dominant, surrendering yourself in whatever capacity you two have decided. You should only submit because it fulfils a need in you to do so—like an ache that just won't go away. Accept that your Dominant knows what's best for you, and that they will care for you—and your domineering behaviour will begin to dissolve.

On Being Manipulative

Being manipulative is right up there with domineering behaviour. And for most, if not all Dominants, it's annoying as hell. Forcing your Dominant to do something they normally wouldn't do, or pushing so hard that they ultimately give in, then you're once again not truly submitting or allowing yourself to submit.

For example, some submissives will tell a Dominant that they need to see this thing, or experience that thing, to feel blah blah blah fucking emotion before they're ready to submit. The Dominant will then find themselves jumping through proverbial hoops to accomplish these things, only to find that the rules have once again changed—and the submissive now needs them to do something else before they submit.

I've heard some submissives say that they're just being persuasive, and that their Dominant doesn't mind their behaviour. I'm willing to bet that if I asked their Dominants, they would say otherwise. Now I'm not saying that a submissive can't change their mind, because as I will mention later in this book, the agreements that a submissive has with their Dominant may change.

Now, if this is something you're doing or have realised you're doing, and every accomplishment only brings more requirements, you might want to take a look at what you're really wanting from your dynamic.

Because while it may likely be that you're unsure of your agreement and need to think on some things, this behaviour will likely be seen as if you're fucking with your Dominant's feelings and manipulating them, simply to see what you can get away with.

Listen, Dominants DO NOT want a submissive that tries to maintain control or bend their will. It's counterproductive to the power exchange, which is the cornerstone of any D/s relationship.

On Being Bratty

And finally, I'd like to talk about being bratty. You'll hear a lot of people saying that they identify as a brat, and I'll be the first to let you know that being a brat is not an identity—It's a mindset, one typically brought on by a state of being, which I'll get into in a bit. But to continue, the term brat (as an identity) was brought on by kinky people who wanted to say they had a Dominant or somehow fit into the BDSM lifestyle, but had no intention of ever really submitting to... Well, anyone.

The term was further popularised by internet communities and websites—FetLife in particular. Newer submissives that were never corrected just assumed being a brat was a thing, and people have ever since been trying to make it one.

Now, there is a HUGE difference between a submissive simply being playful and one exhibiting bratty behaviour. And I don't think that a submissive exhibiting said bratty behaviour always indicates that they are indeed a brat. Oftentimes, a submissive being bratty is just their being playful, exploring the reactions of the Dominant, and toeing the line of what would be considered unacceptable. This is something typically seen in the early stages of a dynamic, whilst the couple is ironing out the intricacies of their respective roles.

A lot of submissives and Dominants alike say that being bratty is okay in a relationship, while in other dynamics, being bratty is just considered playful fun. I'm not against a submissive being a bit playful, as I find it adorable in a lot of cases. But bratty behaviour is never welcome in a submissive. It's just bad form and makes both a submissive and their Dominant look bad.

I consider bratty behaviour to be a submissive's childish attempts to manipulate their Dominant. I've seen some submissives be bratty in ways that make me shake my head and wonder why they were ever accepted as a submissive, or why the Dominant doesn't toss them into oncoming traffic.

With this said, there are times that a submissive will genuinely be going through something they're experiencing difficulty with, and acting out is the only way they can cope with whatever's going on. This is the 'state of being' I mentioned earlier.

I want to take a moment and say this: If you're a submissive reading this, please be aware that while you do have the absolute right to feel anything you happen to be feeling, this in no way gives you a bloody excuse to behave any way you want because of it. There's a difference between acting out and acting like a fucking twat. That's a form of abuse, totally not acceptable, and I'd implore anyone not to deal with that shite. If you're really dealing with that much, I'd suggest having a sit-down with your partner to discuss it.

I'll end all of this by saying once again that a brat is not an identity—it's a mindset. Simple as that. And a true Dominant will always be able to tell the difference between a brat and a playful submissive. Always.

Why is any of this important to know?

Knowing the traits that are detrimental to a submissive's relationship and themselves can bring about the change that is necessary if submission is your goal. The truth is that you can change who you are if you truly want to do that. You're the only person who can. So if submission really is what you want in life, you can make the changes necessary.

However, if you aren't willing to work on these things and you enter into a D/s relationship, then you're not being honest in your intentions to a Dominant. How can you submit if you're not going to make the changes necessary to be a submissive worthy of their control?

Being aware of your non-submissive traits can also help a prospective partner be aware of what they are in for. For example, one of my former submissives was straightforward about her having a lot of personal changes to go through in order to submit in the way she wanted and to be able to give what I wanted from her. I told her that I was willing to work with her while she made the necessary changes.

What Now?

You've made the first step if you can see these traits hindering your submissive attitude and causing trouble for yourself and your partner. Next, you need to start working on changing yourself. This is not an easy process, but it's possible if you wish it. Buy a few self-help books if you need them to help you improve your behaviour and figure out what skills are needed to change your attitude. You can also seek professional help or that of a mentor. Many times, having someone else talk to you about your struggle can bring you closer to shedding those poor behaviours.

If, through all this, you still can't shake those feelings of selfishness and manipulative behaviours, then you've just one admission left—you're not cut out to be submissive.

I've hopefully given you enough to think about to get you started, and as you can see, it's not a dead end. If you're willing to work at it, and it's something you really want, then submission is possible. Good things are never easy to achieve. Work hard at it and you'll be rewarded.

Myths of Being Submissive

'Submissive' is a term that seems to have a lot of negative connotation to it in today's society. A lot of it has absolutely nothing to do with the submission in BDSM dynamics, but when newbies first come across the term, they typically don't know a thing about BDSM, so it can be a bit of a shock for it to be described in regards to BDSM relationships. So I'm going to clear up a few myths about what it means to be submissive in a D/s relationship.

Submissives are weak.

Bullshit. It takes a strong person to choose to submit. The idea that submissives are weak comes from the thought that submissives get walked over and put themselves down, which is quite misogynistic, to be honest.

To be honest, this line of thought comes from people who don't understand the concept of submission. In addition, if you call yourself a people pleaser, or have been called a submissive because of your desire to please others, this doesn't always mean you're submissive in personality—I know a lot of Dominants who are also people pleasers.

To be submissive, you have to be masochistic.

Nope, not the fuck at all. Being in a D/s relationship doesn't mean

a submissive is also into pain, or that they are even remotely masochistic. A strongly submissive person can have a low pain tolerance,
and play sessions that involve pain would honestly do nothing for
that person except for make them not want to do anything—ever.

All submission is sexual.
Negatory. Submission is not always linked with sexuality. I'll say
this on occasion in this book, but BDSM is NOT about sex. It can
be a PART of a BDSM dynamic, but should never be an all-encom-
passing part of a solid relationship—BDSM or otherwise.

Submissives shouldn't have their own opinions.

For fuck's sake, submissives are people, not bloody dogs (Puppy play
doesn't count, silly person). People are full of opinions, viewpoints,
and ways they think on the lives they live—this includes those who
identify as a submissive. If anyone calling themselves knowledgeable
in this lifestyle alludes to this, for your sake, please bow the fuck
out of receiving any further advice from them.

◇◇◇

BDSM Roles: D-Types

D-type roles are just as varied as s-types—and I find most of the
new titles just as ridiculous as the submissive ones. So again, I'm
going to stick the common ones—Dominants, Masters, Tops,
Daddies and Owners.

- **Dominant**: A Dominant is someone who exercises control in
  a D/s relationship. Can be used for either male or female Dominants. By the way, a female Dominant is called a Dominatrix.

- **Master**: A Master is an owner of a slave, or a person highly skilled
  at something—for example, a Master of Ropework.

- **Tops**: A Top is the person in control during a scene or in play, but may or may not be a Dominant.

- **Daddies**: A Daddy is someone who takes on a father role in a relationship and is often, but not always, a Dominant. And yes, there are Mommies, too.

- **Owners**: Owners are those who have possession of another, usually a slave or pet.

On Dominance

Many people assume that a Dominant makes demands and orders at all times. This may of course, happen once the relationship has been established, and there is understanding within the dynamic. But there's a huge element of trust that needs to be built within a relationship with a power dynamic. Even when 'forced' to do something, it should be on the submissive's own free will. There should always be a way to bow out, exit, or safeword available.

BDSM is all about placing your trust in another person. Submissives often take on that role for the sake of surrendering control and giving themselves largely to another person. That said, in a healthy relationship, they will be the ones who ultimately decide when to start and stop. The relationship doesn't work unless the submissive truly has control of themselves, understands that control, and is supported in said control.

◇◇◇

Being Dominant vs. Domineering

'An arrogant man is domineering, while a confident man is dominant.' This is something that I was told a long time ago, by an elder member of my house. And I've never forgotten it.

From those on the outside looking in, Dominants appear to be calling the shots, regardless of what the submissive does or does not want to be doing. But BDSM relationships rarely start at this point, and the submissive is never truly out of control.

For a long time now, I've noticed that more and more people who have found their way into this lifestyle are confused as to the differences between one being Dominant versus domineering. This is usually because of some sort of mis-education. While I've met more than a few people who were nothing more than blatant domineering wankers who shouldn't be in charge of a fucking lamppost, there's enough of a grey area between the two for the distinction to be pretty confusing.

What does it mean to be Domineering?
According to the Merriam-Webster dictionary, the definition of domineering is one 'inclined to exercise arbitrary and overbearing control over others'.

Those who are domineering use force to gain control over a submissive, rather than gaining submission by earning it. A domineering person will often use some kind of threat to assert their will, as they typically have no other way to enforce it. Therefore, people do what they want to avoid some kind of adverse outcome.

Being domineering is usually based on these insecurities and/or a total lack of trust. Because of these insecurities, domineering people can't even trust those who love them. They don't love themselves and are incapable of accepting the love of others.

What does it mean to be Dominant?
The word Dominant is defined as 'commanding, controlling, or prevailing over all others, again according to Merriam-Webster dictionary. In contrast to the domineering person above, a Dominant person most often inspires others to do what they ask—and these

people want to do these things asked to please them.

The role of a Dominant is as much mentor and guide as anything else. A true Dominant is one who takes charge. Their submissive is their responsibility, and they understand this. They take into consideration what is best for their submissive. It's what drives them, and in turn becomes one of the many things that makes their submissive want to please them.

For example, I can go to my submissive and simply look in her eyes and calmly speak a command, and she knows exactly what is expected of her because I have already trained her to know (to be honest, I've always had rather brilliant submissives for the most part). She knows exactly what would happen if she decided against it, and can make that decision in an educated way.

But more than anything, she will obey my commands because she respects me, because she enjoys doing things that she knows will please me. And while it's possible that I may intimidate her, she knows she has absolutely no reason to fear me. I control her because I am a person deserving of her servitude.

Ultimately, dominance isn't about size, or force, or how loud you become when angry. It's about being in control of yourself and the ability to control another in a way that makes them happy to serve you. A good Dominant never leaves their submissive feeling bad about themselves. Even if they're into humiliation, they've a responsibility to pay attention to and take care of their submissives' mental and emotional states, because constant humiliation is nothing more than abuse.

What do you think your role is?
Now with the definitions of D-types and s-types out of the way, how do you decide what fits you the best? If you're trying to decide

whether you're a Dominant or submissive, try taking the BDSM Test at bdsmtest.org. Though I don't agree with some of the titles that it gives in them, the results are extremely detailed and will be a great way to spark conversation with your current or potential play partners.

◇◇◇

Gorean Relationships

I mentioned Gorean relationships earlier as an example of a slave relationship, and I also touched on Gor back in Chapter 2, but I figured I'd explain it in a bit more detail. Gorean, or 'Gor,' is a BDSM lifestyle based on the Gor series, a set of fiction books written by John Norman. The relationships are typically Master/slave, and the participants often adhere to the culture, rituals, and protocols depicted in the books, such as the slave positions that the slave (known as a kajira) must assume, specific commands that are taught and followed, and guidelines for dress.'

The Gorean lifestyle and teachings are WAY too in-depth for me to try and explain in this book, so I'll stick to the 'typical' relationship built upon it.

In Gor, slaves are usually required to address all free men and women as Master/Mistress, and whilst a slave may be owned by one person, s/he is at the will of his/her Master, and can be loaned or 'sold' to another or released if the Master so decides.

Whilst Gorean relationships are often built upon an owner/property Master/slave dynamic, and would be discontinued without it, the relationships more often than not include love, care, affection, etc, as well they should.

Other aspects of Gorean relationships include the fact that a slave is expected to obey anyone whom their Master chooses, and the only other option to obedience is for the slave to beg for reprieve or release. I've only met a few people who truly adhere to this, though such practice is followed by most people in the Gor community.

Essentially, it's the goal of a kajira to please at all times. They're often not allowed to refer to themselves as 'I, me, or mine', and instead refer to themselves in ways such as 'this girl'.

While it's understood that a kajira is to obey without question, we

Fig. 2.1.: The Kajira Emblem 'Kef'

all know that if we don't maintain something properly, its reliability lessens. Some liken this to servicing your car. If you don't, eventually things don't work as well. This is true for a kajira. Underneath their slavery and service is a human being. They have personal goals, feelings and needs. It may be at their Master's discretion when, if at all, his slave gets these (affection, attention, etc.), but to refuse a slave these things would likely leave them with a slave who has little desire or incentive to be a good one.

Gorean relationships are on the extreme end of service and obedience, but it's important that while many Gor lifestyles preach the need to be limitless slaves and entirely dominant Masters, they're all still people, and many don't go to such an extent that they disregard their property's welfare. There is still a great deal of emotion in Gorean relationships. Many are based on love, care and honour for one another—as well they should be.

Chapter 5:

ON POLYAMORY AND KINKSTERS

I know a lot of people who have never felt completely comfortable in monogamous relationships—myself included. They've wondered about the differences between monogamy and polyamory, whether or not they could actually have relationships with more than one person, and if what they really want is to be polyamorous.

◇◇◇

Let's Chat About Polyamory

You'll likely hear a LOT of people talking about polyamory in conversations you have, as you become more involved in this lifestyle. And I've noticed that a lot of people are either conflating open relationships and polyamory, or aren't polyamorous at all but saying that they are, as a way to sleep around and shag the masses without any perceived guilt, or even actually wanting to be in a relationship—none of which is fair to truly polyamorous people.

This was largely brought on by the swinger community, who discovered that they could find more people to shag simply by saying that they were Dominants or submissives. As you grow in this lifestyle, you'll discover a lot of couples looking for 'thirds', 'unicorns', etc. Now, some of them may genuinely be looking for other partners to be in a relationship with. But for the most part, they're likely just using the person for nothing more than a way to spice up their relationship—A glorified fuck toy, if you will.

If you're genuinely polyamorous, I would highly suggest doing your research when dealing with couples—or, for that matter, anyone else claiming to be polyamorous. They'll usually target newbies, having the woman initiate a conversation, who later introduces them to the guy. After this, they'll do a tag team conversation, which usually consists of a lot of mind fuckery, asking a lot of questions to find out what exactly they might be able to get away with, slowly drawing the person into their circle—or triangle, in this case.

The relationships will usually end after they become bored with the person, slowly casting them aside to find someone new, which is again not fair to truly polyamorous people, because they thrive on the connections they make with the people whom they choose to love, and believe love them back. If these connections are found to be false or are suddenly broken, truly polyamorous people can find themselves feeling lost, with thoughts of 'what did I do wrong?' or 'is there something wrong with me?' bouncing about in their heads.

If you've found yourself feeling this way, I'll be the first to let you know, you probably didn't do anything. You were likely just duped, used, and dumped. People can be dicks like that, and it fucking sucks. However, while it does indeed sting and will leave a pain that feels like it won't ever go away, I guarantee that you'll recover. Just learn from the situation, and keep your wits about you so it doesn't happen again. Try not to let it make you become cynical, though.

There are also guys that try to build a harem of submissives under the guise of polyamory. But these blokes are just doing it to project some form of bravado to their communities and gain some form of notoriety from it.

While I have met a few guys who genuinely love and care for the people in said harem, it's a rarity to see it done properly. So again, I encourage you to do your research when or if these blokes approach you as well.

In either of these cases, remember that communication will always be your greatest tool when dealing with... Tools, I suppose. I'm sure you've noticed my constant mentioning of doing your research in this book. And if you haven't, you will. Communication is a part of this.

◇◇◇

Wait, back up a second... What the fuck is a Unicorn?

A horse—typically white in colour—with a bloody horn protruding from its head. A land-lubbing Narwhal, if you will.

In all seriousness, a unicorn in polyamorous or swinging lifestyles is usually a bisexual single female who is willing to have sex with or enter a relationship with an established couple. Although unicorns are usually female, the term can apply to someone of any gender.

In swinging, a unicorn is a woman who has sex with both partners, no strings or drama attached. In polyamorous setups, a unicorn may be expected to join a closed triad—meaning she won't date anyone outside of the three-person relationship.

Since these folks are rare, they're likened to the mythical unicorn.

So what is Polyamory, exactly?

By definition, polyamory is consensual non-monogamy between two or more people, where all parties are aware of each other's existence, and open communication is present across all relationships. Polyamory challenges the idea that loving more than one person means loving each of them less.

In practice, everyone involved agrees to allow each other to date, have sex with, and cultivate meaningful relationships with multiple people. It's not uncommon to have multiple partners and be deeply committed to each of them. The operative word here is relationship.

But as of late, polyamory has become a blanket term that people use to describe many different types of relationships. Other terms used for these relationships include: polyfidelity, open marriages, open relationships, open dating, friends with benefits, triads, quads, vees, and communities.

Saying this, it *really* needs to be understood that polyamory is not the same as group sex, kink, swinging, or casual sleeping around. Polyamorous and monogamous people alike can do those things if they want—but those activities are separate from the structure of polyamorous relationships.

Whether you've toyed with the idea of polyamory for years or just recently felt it might be right for you, there are a few things to sort out first—so you can give yourself a fair chance to see if this path truly fits.

◇◇◇

What's Your Motivation?
If you are searching for a lifestyle that works for you, and your ideal happens to involve more than one partner in a relationship, then

that's great. However, simply trying to find a bandage for problems within your relationship (or wanting an excuse to see other people) isn't the right reason for going into a polyamorous lifestyle.

If you're trying to fix a 'broken' relationship by adding more people, that's really not a good reason either, and from my experience, never really ends well. However, people who have struggled in traditional monogamous relationships might find polyamory appealing.

If it's more of a personal preference, rather than simply you and/ or your partner trying to improve things via a new person, then it's more likely you'll actually enjoy polyamory rather than just feeling obligated to adapt to it.

What Do You Want Your Poly Relationship to Look Like?

Like I mentioned before, there are all kinds and combinations of polyamorous relationships, including polyfidelity, open marriages, open relationships, triads, and others. This is one of the appealing things about polyamorous relationships for many people: they're less rigid in guidelines and expectations than monogamous relationships typically are.

Still, it's crucial to ask:

- How will casual dating be handled?
- What are the sexual safety expectations?
- What happens if you fall in love with multiple people?
- These preferences might evolve, but having a starting point will help guide your choices.

Do you get jealous, or are you possessive?

Jealousy is a totally normal thing for just about anyone. And polyamorous people aren't immune to jealousy, either. Being overly possessive is never a positive thing, either, but in a polyamorous relationship, it's especially stressful.

When jealousy does occur within polyamorous relationships, it's usually discussed. The person feeling jealous should figure out what's bothering them and which of their needs aren't being met. Then they, and any partners, can negotiate boundaries.

When you have feelings for somebody, it's difficult to not get a bit stressed when they're flirting with or show interest in another person. However, if you can't push past that jealousy to have a clear-headed conversation about it in an attempt to become comfortable with it, then polyamory probably isn't for you.

Are you willing to be completely honest?

In healthy monogamous relationships, there's usually nothing to lie about—partners generally agree on boundaries that include sexual exclusivity.

However, in polyamory, things can get trickier. Introducing another person can be a bit rocky at first, but and communication are absolutely essential between all parties involved.

If you don't feel like you can be 100% truthful with your partners—especially about new connections—then that's a warning sign. If, however, you genuinely believe you can abide by the rules of being honest with your partner, and communicating openly with them, then a polyamorous lifestyle may be a great choice for you and your love life.

My Thoughts on Kinksters

I've noticed over the past few years that the line between kink and BDSM has become a bit blurred. If you're new to BDSM, and wondering if BDSM is a thing you're really wanting to be part of, I'll give my two cents for you to think on about kinksters—people that are simply kinky—as you might simply be a person that wants to experience the kinky desires you've discovered, and not necessarily a person that wants to go any further beyond having those needs met.

As I was taught, the difference is this:
BDSM has an implied power exchange. Kink does not.

It's really that simple.

It's also worth pointing out that not everyone who claims to be a Dominant or submissive actually is one. Plenty of people are just kinky in some way—and that's perfectly valid.

There are kinky friends of mine who claim there is 'no such thing as a power exchange'. They use the argument that, 'You cannot legally consent to be someone's slave. ' Sure, maybe not legally—but when I see a slave serving their Owner, it's obvious that they are in an M/s dynamic. I have yet to hear a slave tell their Master or Mistress, 'Get your own fucking beer, ' as I have with kinky vanilla couples.

D/s relationships vary widely—from 24/7 dynamics, to weekend arrangements, to one-off sessions, and everything in between. But where a power exchange is present, the relationship moves from simple kink into the realm of BDSM.

To be a kinkster doesn't mean that you're part of the BDSM lifestyle, but if you're part of the BDSM lifestyle, then it definitely makes you a kinkster as well.

If you find you're simply a kinkster, there's absolutely nothing wrong with that. However, be honest with your partner—especially if they're looking for something deeper. That falls under that whole 'communication' thing I keep banging on about.

In a strictly kink-based relationship, anything goes. And yes—it can be far more exciting than anything vanilla. But like I said earlier, kinksters are often just exploring their desires because it's fun—not because they want to go any further.

So, to recap:

- Being a kinkster doesn't make you part of the BDSM lifestyle.
- But if you're into BDSM, you're definitely a kinkster too.
- If you're just kinky, that's absolutely fine—but be upfront about it, especially if your partner is looking for something deeper.

Without a power exchange, kink is just that—kink. I'll talk more about power exchange in a bit.

Chapter 6:

MEETING KINKY PEEPS

One of the more difficult things for newbies to do is find other lifestylers in their area. Most people aren't going around advertising that they're kinky or a lifestyler, and it's not like it comes up in general conversation, typically because people don't want to 'out' themselves and run the risk of having people say something like, 'oh, you're one of those', or stop speaking to you altogether. It's not a good feeling, believe me.

◇◇◇

Understanding Kinky Connections

Now I'm sure you already know this, but finding a kinky partner is significantly different from finding a vanilla partner. Even if you don't know this, anyone will tell you that it's totally true.

There are a couple of ways you can go about doing this. You can go to a munch, directly to a kink-related event, or meet someone online. I don't ever suggest that total newbies ever immediately go to a kink-related event, be it at a club, dungeon, or house event (where you don't know anyone, or completely trust the person that invited you to have your best interests in mind), because kink events are not something I believe anyone should simply dive into uninformed. You could find yourself stranded somewhere with total strangers whilst virtually naked, because the person that brought you to said location turned out to be a total fucking baby man. This is a real thing that happened to someone, and I'd rather it not happen to you.

After you've got some knowledge under your belt, I most certainly suggest checking out a few kink-related events. When you go to kinky events, your chances of forming friendships increase, as well as your odds of finding a like-minded partner. Not only are friendships in the BDSM community a healthy thing, but you're statistically more likely to meet a partner through others in the community than any other means. Once people trust you, they'll typically be happy to introduce you to other kinky friends with whom they think you're compatible.

With all this said, I'll be covering going to munches and online dating, because these are better options than, as I mentioned, immediately going to a kinky event or club.

Or they should be, at least. Anyway, you ready?

◇◇◇

Finding Kinky People at Munches

If you're honestly looking for like-minded people, then you should get off your arse and go where the kinksters are. Seriously, get the fuck out of the house. It seems that nowadays, most people trying to find other kinky people spend all of their time behind a computer or on their phones, almost religiously refusing to get out of the house and meet people.

Don't get me wrong, dating sites are indeed a feasible way to find potential partners, but it's better to use the internet as nothing more than a tool to find other kinky people in your area. With this said, my advice is to attend a munch or two in your area, which will definitely allow you to meet some possibly like-minded people.

◇◇◇

So What's a Munch, Anyway?

A munch is a gathering of kinky people in a vanilla setting, usually a pub or cafe. You don't have to worry about being outed, as munches look like a business or hobby group meet-up. There is a lot of socialising, friendly conversation, and eating. Since munches are held at vanilla venues, and there is no play allowed, the focus can be more on social interaction, which is excellent for newbies. This means that you'll have plenty of opportunities to talk to people and get to know them. Munches are also a fantastic place to find out about other events happening in your area.

Munches are a helpful part of the BDSM community because people can go to meet other like-minded people, to see old friends, and to establish themselves in the community. If you want to attend some of the private parties that are held in your city, you'll want to start at a munch where people can get to know you. People who host parties want to see that you can behave appropriately in a social setting, and get to know you a bit before inviting you to their private homes or dungeons.

Munches also offer a chance to figure out if this part of the community is right for you. Keep in mind that different munches draw different people, so if you aren't crazy about the first one you attend, try another until you find the right fit.

One more thing: Because jargon can be a barrier to first-time attendees of a munch, you should try to understand the terms listed back in Chapter 3, so that you'll be able to speak more knowledgeably about BDSM, and to understand what's being said around you.

◇◇◇

How Do I Find a Munch?

To be honest, the internet is the best way to find kinky groups if you know where to look. However, doing a search for 'kink events' will likely not do much good. This is because most kink events don't promote themselves outside of specific sites. There are a few places you can do this, but the one that most people use is FetLife. Just do a search on the 'Events' page for your area.

Who Can Attend a Munch?

Normally, anyone can attend a munch that hasn't specifically been blacklisted from a group or location. Most munches don't have any sort of screening process, but some do.

No Play at the Munch

Most munches do not normally include play because the idea of a munch is to have a space where people can freely socialise, and so that new people can specifically attend without needing to be vetted, without having a fear that some sort of play will occur, or that they must participate in anything other than casual conversation with others. As such, leave your toys and other fetish gear outside. This is a social event, not a place to conduct a scene.

What Do I Wear to a Munch?

Consider your typical, casual attire to be appropriate. Discreet collars and some black is generally accepted, but a high degree of fetish wear (leather harnesses, ball gags, etc.) at a non-fetish establishment can (and typically will) cause social problems and even a loss of the ability to host a munch at that particular establishment.

General Munch Etiquette

Just because you're around kinky people, this shouldn't change the fact that you should behave at a munch in the same way you would if you were at any other type of social gathering. This means being polite and respectful. Because if you're not, you'll likely not be invited to or told about other events.

With this said, while protocols will vary from one munch to another, these protocols will apply to just about any munch you're attending:

Respect the confidentiality of the event: Do not ever compromise someone's anonymity regarding kink (aka 'outing someone') or take pictures of people at a munch. That's a quick way to make sure you're not invited to other events.

Because of the confidentiality of the event, do not request probing information about someone's personal details, such as where they work, where they live, what their real name is, etc., as that can give a bad impression. It's fine if they volunteer these things, but it's generally not a good idea to probe for this information.

Be friendly and respectful to others, and treat people as people: There may be people who enjoy objectification and being thought of as a sex object. But you still need to build trust and friendship before you can ever approach those sorts of relationship dynamics with them.

Be courteous and respectful to your waitstaff, and be sure to tip well: If you don't, the munch coordinators may not be invited to host another event at that establishment, which wouldn't be a good thing.

Be very wary of consent violations: The one that people seem to stuff up is touching. Do NOT touch another person without asking. I mean hugging someone, but you will find some people who won't even shake hands with you. However, I don't believe you have to ask for a handshake—that's just bloody ridiculous.

Best practices indicate asking before touching someone, and asking if a worn necklace is a collar or not and what its significance may be, as these are typical potential pitfalls. If someone violates your consent, be sure to tell them. If they continue to violate your consent or attempt to do so, consider sharing this with the munch coordinator.

Exchanging personal information: Be sure not to give away highly personal details about yourself right away, such as your real name, address, phone number, and other information. As a matter of fact, I wouldn't advise you to do that after immediately meeting someone anywhere (which I talk a bit about later), but what do I know? Consider using an online handle or profile name to exchange information to start communicating with others to protect yourself.

Red Flags and Politics: Not everyone is going to give you the best advice or have an established reputation. If you aren't sure about someone, give it some time, and they will begin to show more of themselves to you. Not every report about someone having a bad or good reputation is accurate. Some people may have alternate motives you may not immediately notice. Give it a bit of time, which will help you figure these things out.

Mind your business: Sometimes, you might see or hear a couple doing or saying things that get under your skin, and you might feel like you have to defend someone's honour, unless you personally know them and their dynamic, or someone is screaming bloody murder and asking for help, shut the fuck up and keep your comments to yourself.

Do NOT get involved. You're not going to appear a rescuer, or saviour of any kind. You'll likely just make yourself look like some twat that got in the middle of a couple's dynamic.

I will say this, if it bothers you that much, and it seems like it might become something that might threaten others at the munch, or it appears to be something that might get the munch shut down, bring it to the attention of the munch leader or organiser.

Swarming: New members of a munch may experience swarming, where they receive lots of attention from many people all at once, which can be overwhelming. This, however, typically applies to females. And the more attractive you are, the worse it is. If you think this might be something that might happen for you, you might consider attending the munch with a friend. Just don't be a dick, because I can guarantee that you're not the first attractive person to attend a munch, and you won't be last.

Now, the flip side to swarming is that some new people may also be entirely ignored. This is because a lot of people at munches can be a bit clique-ish (because they didn't get enough of this shite in secondary school). If no one seems to greet you, you're probably just going to have to open up a conversation with others or talk to the munch coordinator. They'll likely introduce you to a few people to get you started.

◇◇◇

Finding Kinky People on Dating Sites

So you've decided to skip going to munches and check out dating sites and apps instead, huh? Like I mentioned, the best way to find other kinky people is to actually go out and meet them in person. But if you're still on the fence about meeting people in person, no worries, because you're not alone. There are a lot of people who go the online route. There are a few situations where meeting people online may be the better option. For example, they may want to avoid going to live events due to employment or legal concerns, or they may live in an area without easy access to a kink community.

I talked about using FetLife to find a munch, which, in and of itself, is all fine and dandy. But if you're looking for a place to meet kinky people to be in a relationship with, FetLife isn't designed for meeting people. It's really just a social media site—like Facebook for kinky people. You can't search for users the way you can on a dating site, like being able to search by common factors, such as location or age. Hell, it doesn't even let you search by kink-specific criteria, like whether you're looking for a Dominant or Top, submissive or bottom, etc. Needless to say, it's honestly annoying as all hell.

Another problem is that finding quality people from FetLife is akin to finding a needle in a haystack, dirt in a snowstorm, my liver after getting arseholed on the weeken--

Ahem. You erm... You get the picture.

With this said, there are loads of dating websites made specifically for kinky people. Years ago, I was using CollarSpace, which was a popular option for a lot of people back then. There are loads of other options available now, but from what I've found, most of the other websites out there all seem to charge ridiculous amounts of money to use the site. In my opinion, this is total bullshit, and I for one am NOT paying for a kink dating website. But I'm also cheap—because frugality is a thing, and I have bills to pay, dammit. Anyway, for this reason, a lot of people stick to sites like CollarSpace and FetLife—which, as I mentioned, isn't a dating site. But they don't cost anything to use.

And before you say anything, I know that running a website costs money, and people should be paid for their work. I, however, don't think these websites are run by lifestylers, because there's a difference between being paid for your work, and taking advantage of or blatantly pocket raping people—especially MY people. But this is a whole different discussion altogether, so erm... Let's continue.

Now, the main benefit of kinky dating sites is that you can typically get some sort of idea of your sexual and kink compatibility with a potential partner, just by looking at their profile. And people on these sites are more likely to be open to upfront conversations about kink, or sex in general.

There are a few things I'd like to let you know before you decide to go jumping pelvis-first into something (or onto someone) you might later regret. A few do's and don'ts as it were. I feel like I would be doing you a disservice by not touching on the subject of online dating. ESPECIALLY if you met someone on FetLife, or any other kink-related website, for that matter.

Now, while I'm sure that most of what I'm going to say is common sense—or it should be, in any case—it needs to be said. I've met more than enough people who throw caution to the wind, just to have something dodgy happen to them because they chose not to be careful. So if none of what I'm saying pertains to you, then congratulations on not being a complete idiot.

I should also let you know that I'm writing this more for those of you who are actually looking for an actual relationship with someone. I'm looking at you, fuckboys.

◇◇◇

Do's and Don'ts of Online Dating

DO decide up front what distance you're willing to travel. If a potential partner lives too far away, the growth of the relationship will only go so far, being capped by the amount the two of you are able and willing to travel.

Keep in mind that there are some people who look for distant relationships specifically to keep a relationship from growing beyond a certain level. If this is you, or you feel that your relationship isn't growing, then it's best to either not become involved, or end the relationship—hopefully amicably.

DO move your conversation from messaging to phone calls. Some people are great writers, can even have a friend feed them lines or ghostwrite for them (à la Cyrano de Bergerac). In a phone conversation, you'll get a better sense of whether your personalities click, if they've really as much knowledge about this lifestyle as they claim.

DON'T let your discussion of the kinks on your profile take away from actually having a fucking conversation. While BDSM may be a part of your life, it shouldn't be the ONLY thing in your life. You're likely a bit anxious to get across that you're into BDSM, and I get that. But unless all you're looking for is a fuck buddy or a play partner, it's far too easy to make it look like kink is the only thing you've got going on in your life. You should want to show women that you're a man of substance. The operative word here is man.

DON'T immediately start talking about all the sex and kink things you're into. Honesty is a great thing, but once again, unless all you're looking for is a fuck buddy or a play partner, there is such a thing as 'too much, too soon'. Subtle hints are better than 'this is me, take it or leave it'.

DON'T choose your dates solely based on photos. I'm laughing at this one, because most of the photos you'll find will be dick pics, anyway. With this said, if someone is actually worth your time, they'll have more going for their profiles than pictures of their Pretty Ricky (Tricky Dicky? Nixon? Mr President? Fuck it, you know what I mean).

DO stay on high alert. If someone sounds too good to be true, they just might be. Now I'm not saying that you should be desperately cynical whilst scrolling through potential dates, but it's helpful to be realistic, keeping your guard up until someone you've met can prove they are who they say they are.

DON'T disclose where you live, or any personal information that could lead to where you live. While most people who use online dating sites are probably just as normal as you are, it's always best to err on the side of caution when meeting someone new—especially when meeting someone from a kink site. And this applies to whether you've met them online or not.

DON'T put your face in your profile, or send photos of yourself before getting to know someone. I've heard stories of people who will chat you up and ask for a photo, just for you to send it and either never hear from them again or find yourself being asked for more photos. Now you've given your photo to who-the-fuck-knows, to end up who-the-fuck-knows-where. I've been part of a few of these stories, and that shit isn't cool. So if this isn't something you're okay with having happen to you, save yourself the anxiety, and either obscure your face or crop it out altogether.

If someone chooses to send you a photo, so fucking what? What THEY choose to do has absolutely nothing to do with YOUR level of comfort.

I know that you may feel like you're running the risk of missing out on this 'awesome person', but you'll honestly save yourself the headache of dealing with someone that's simply some wank photo collector. If you think they're that awesome, then arrange to meet them in person, which eliminates the photo collector thing. If they persist, then you're better off cutting ties. With this said...

DO post a recent photo of yourself, if you're okay with having your face out there. It's rather annoying to go through all the trouble and time of chatting someone up, just to meet them in person, to have them look absolutely nothing like the photo that they have posted online, or was taken fifteen years ago.

DON'T try to put up a front about who you are, pretend to be something you're not, or exaggerate your knowledge or skill within this lifestyle. There are far too many wannabes out there as is—especially on the D-type side. Why would you even want to be that person, anyway? Anyone who's been part of this lifestyle will be able to tell that you've little to no clue of what you're doing, and will totally call you on your bullshit. Maybe not to your face, but it'll happen. And word tends to get around fast. Now, this doesn't mean you can't experiment or that you aren't free to change your mind, but be real about what you know.

DON'T post dick pics. This is for the guys reading this book. I want to take a moment to let you know something: As tempting as it may be, posting a photo of your little fuck buddy is a bad fucking idea. It isn't attractive. Remember that 'man of substance' thing I mentioned? It applies here, and doesn't just apply to men, you get me?

Seriously, it suggests that you honestly believe that it's the absolute most important thing about you, and that's just plain stupid. I don't give a damn how endowed you are, or think you are, it's not something that anyone wants to see. No one worth your giving a toss is going to want to see your Magic Johnson (hahaha, I did it again. But fuck it, you know what I mean). And the people who do want to see it are likely WAY more trouble than they're worth.

DO take rejection well. It will happen—and you do not want to appear a fucking twat or get a reputation for being a fucking twat, because you can't handle rejection. Cordiality is always a welcome thing.

And finally, **DON'T** be an arsehole.

◇◇◇

Dealing with New Play Partners

If you've met a new BDSM partner—or someone you hope will be a BDSM partner—you'll want to make sure you'll be safe, especially if you're in the submissive role. There are steps that you should take to stay safe in any dating encounter. Though kink itself isn't dangerous, encounters with kinky people carry risks that are rarely found in vanilla encounters. So here are a few suggestions, which I hope will help you avoid disappointment, things ending in disaster, or you ending up on a milk carton.

Do Some Research

If your potential partner has a profile on a kinky site like FetLife, do a bit of digging. How much experience does it seem like this person has? What events have they gone to? Take a look at their pictures. What kinds of play have they done? What do their other partners have to say about past play sessions? While I don't suggest stalking them, you should look for warning signs. Is there anything on their profile that blatantly opposes things they've told you?

Don't friend people on your potential partner's profile, or contact those people without prior consent from your potential partner. That's wrong, creepy as all hell, and will likely immediately make you seem a stalker.

If you've been going to kink events, you will probably meet or already know people who have seen your potential partner play. Talk to these people. Will they vouch for your potential partner's safety and experience? Compare the things you hear with what your potential partner says, and make your decision from there.

I would suggest talking to people who aren't all in the same circle, as they may collectively be trying to discredit someone they don't like. But under no circumstance should you play with the person until you feel comfortable, and remember that coercion falls under mental fuckery and is not considered consent.

The best way to tell how someone may treat you is how they've treated their other romantic and play partners. Don't be afraid to ask your potential partner for references. This isn't an uncommon request in the kink community. Most kinksters will provide references for you without hesitation, even if it's only one.

While there may be instances where people don't want to be used as a reference, it's doubtful that EVERYONE will have a problem with it. So if you find that you're getting excuses instead of references, you should be concerned.

Be sure that you confirm with your potential partner that the reference is someone they've actually played with, and not just someone they gave as a character reference.

Always meet in public.

When meeting a new potential play partner, always meet in a public place, just for a chat, until you have both gotten to know each other better. A noisy fetish club doesn't count. Don't meet in some dirty pub at night. You need to communicate properly, so you should meet in a relatively quiet and well-lit public place during the daytime. (Lunchtime is good, as it gives you a good excuse to leave if you need it.) You may also want to wait until you trust them before giving them your address to pick you up or drop you off.

Make it clear that you won't play at the first meeting. If you feel you need to be careful, don't give out your phone number yet. Use an anonymous form of contact, or create a private email address just for this sort of thing.

If you then agree to play at a later time, you'll both need a form of contact that is not anonymous. I've found it easier to just have each other's phone numbers, at the very least. If your playing is going to just be a one-off, then it's okay to stick with anonymity, because no one needs a clingy psycho bugging the piss out of them.

Have a safe call in place.
You should definitely have a friend to act as a safe call for the first time meeting, at least. They should know where you're meeting and how long you'll be there with them. Tell the Dominant this. If they are not OK with it, walk away.

Call your friend before you play and tell them the address. If they meet you in a vehicle, then get their tag number and call it in to your safe call person before getting into the bloody car. Tell your safe call exactly when you'll call again after you part company with the Dominant. If they don't get your second call, they should alert the police. Never be embarrassed to call the police. If you need to do it, do it.

Don't let anyone make you feel guilty about wanting to be safe.
If your date gives you a hard time about your safety measures for your first meet-up, unless they're just teasing you about the ridiculousness of online dating, they are likely a fuckboy. Do yourself a favour, and don't put up with that nonsense. Just get yourself

out of that situation as soon as possible—maybe by having your safe call fake an emergency, or saying something like, 'I think I left my house burning'.

◇◇◇

Red Flags to Watch for in a Potential Dominant

So you've met someone? Awesomeness, I knew you had it in you! Actually, not really, I have no sodding idea who the hell you are.

Anyway, looking for a Dominant for the first time can be challenging, to say the least. You should definitely be watching out for red flags to avoid putting yourself in danger. Typically, new submissives suffer from 'submissive frenzy' or 'sub frenzy', where they want to do 'all the things'. However, when you're looking for a Dominant, things can go really wrong, really fucking fast. Believe me, I've heard more than one horror story of someone who was abused by, or injured by a careless 'Dominant', or one that didn't care at all. It's saddening, but it happens.

Because safety is one of the pillars of BDSM, here are a few red flags to watch out for.

◇◇◇

I'm a Real Dom!

If you get a message from someone who claims to be a 'real Dom' who is looking for a 'real sub' you should have a real look at what they're really saying.

The idea of 'realness' in BDSM is a very dangerous concept. It puts unrealistic expectations on behaviour and doesn't allow for personality, triggers and personal preferences. It's as if this so-called Dominant is trying to put BDSM in a box that fits everyone—or at least every person with whom he or she interacts. Newbies sometimes also use this language to try to appear more experienced than they really are.

Here's how to debunk this red flag: ask what 'real' means to them and how they work with a submissive's personal limits and preferences. If your potential Dominant avoids the question or says something like 'a real submissive will do anything I want to', you should walk away.

I'm officially tired of the word 'real'. Just saying.

I Want to Meet You Now!

Also known as a 'pusher', this type of Dominant is probably just looking to see if you can be easily pressured into doing something. They'll insist on meeting you straightaway, even if you say you need time to chat and get to know them. They'll say, 'Sure, take all the time you need,' but will pressure you in subtle ways, with show tickets, exclusive events, or even by telling you they're leaving for a while and want to meet you before they go.

This type of Dominant makes you wonder: Is this person really interested in you or in getting laid as quickly as possible? Those who insist on meeting you privately, at their place or in a hotel room, etc., are especially dangerous.

So you're probably wondering, 'How do I determine whether a Dominant is just eager or a creep?' This is easy enough: Make him wait until you're ready. If he immediately stops talking to you, you'll know. If he keeps in touch and accepts your decision? Well, that might be a person worth meeting.

Even still, do NOT meet anyone for the first time in a non-public area. That's just fucking mad.

I would like to say this: By 'making him wait', I don't mean a bloody year, or even a few months. The most should be a month or two, if you're constantly talking to each other. 'Being shy' can only be a viable excuse for so long. So if you're not 'ready' by then, you're likely just stringing them along for the sake of feeling desired, or you're hiding something. Which makes you a dick in my opinion.

I Don't Like the Community!

'Not liking the community' can at times be a legitimate thing. Some people are afraid to be outed, and others just don't like the public scene. However, it can also be a sign that they have been (or would be) kicked out of the community for a number of (possibly abusive) reasons. It means the person has been involved in it once and decided not to involve themselves anymore. If they don't like the community just because they know they wouldn't be welcome there, that's a real issue—and a big red flag.

A BDSM community is necessary to learn things and improve both technical and emotional skills. So if a person refuses all contact with your local community, unless the person is from a different community altogether, you should really ask yourself what they know and where they learnt it.

If you're faced with this excuse, ask the Dominant to meet in public. Maybe not necessarily at a munch, but at least in a public setting. If they refuse, cut all contact. People who insist on meeting in private are usually dangerous.

Call Me Master

I previously mentioned people not having others call them by any sort of title before anything was negotiated. And while that might be hot in a role playing setting, if you truly want to have a relationship with a safe Dominant, having someone ask to be called 'Master' before you've developed any kind of trust is a definite red flag.

Seriously, you should be thinking 'We just met, my dude. So... no.'

This also goes for anyone that calls themselves any sort of 'title as a name'. I've met people who call themselves Goddess this, Mistress or Master that. They think they're slick, and a clear sign of a wannabe, in my opinion. It's just another way to see what they can make someone do. Remember, you're not in a dynamic with them, so you don't have to refer to them that way.

These people are usually driven by the idea of ownership, rather than by its reality. They are aware that new submissives are likely to fall for someone who exerts authority right away. But beware: People like this are often driven by some sort of porn-fuelled fantasy rather than reality.

So before you start calling them whatever they want to be called, ask them what their expectations are for the relationship. How much control do they want to have over you? Can you keep going to work or to school? Can you still see your family and friends? If their expectations seem a bit too extreme, it's because they are extreme. If they clarify and they seem reasonable, then you may have grounds for further discussion. Use your instincts here.

I mentioned back in Chapter 4 that submission is something that must be earned in a D/s relationship, and this can be negotiated for scenes as well. However, if you find someone who wants to push you into a 24/7 D/s relationship almost immediately, this can be a real sign of trouble.

I Want to Mentor You!

Like I said back in Chapter 1, I think mentors are awesome. They help you navigate a community that's likely new to you, and they are a useful resource for learning the etiquette and language of BDSM. That said, some people will attempt to take advantage of you under the guise of mentorship.

These people are especially dangerous. They approach you as mentors, gain your trust and begin to influence you in ways that may not be especially healthy. They'll criticise everyone who approaches you, wanting to make sure that they are the only ones you can count on. You come to depend on them, and then they can take full advantage of you.

To make sure that your potential mentor has good intentions, you should lay out two simple rules: no play and no sex. A real mentor wouldn't want these things anyway, and any mentor worth their salt knows this as well, so if they refuse, you know where they stand. If they accept and they keep their word, you'll likely develop a very strong bond based on trust and respect. And this is what BDSM is all about.

Look, when delving into the world of BDSM and other kinky relationships, it's easy to get caught up in desire and fantasy. However, it should be understood that there are real things at stake here. Namely, your overall safety, which includes your life. You should definitely ALWAYS be doing your best to keep your head clear when assessing potential relationships, especially with blokes who display one of the behaviours I've mentioned.

◇◇◇

A Huge Mistake When Meeting Kinky People

One of the biggest mistakes I see new people to kink both meeting in-person or online is engaging someone in an inappropriate way without their permission. While the person you're talking to might identify as a submissive, they're not YOUR submissive, so don't act like it.

If you identify as a D-type, don't expect the cute submissive you just met to call you Grand Master Twat Waffle (or whatever stupid title you created for yourself), or expect them to kneel at your feet. If you identify as an s-type, don't act like you're any and everyone's damned submissive, or approach someone and address them as Master or Mistress.

In either case, you didn't EARN these things from these people. You're engaging them in a kinky activity without negotiating or receiving their consent. Just don't do it. Ever. It will likely invite problems from other people who I doubt you'd want for yourself later, especially from s-types, and especially if things go awry. I'm looking at you, predators.

I also want to clarify something that can cause a bit of confusion at first, which falls under minding your own business at a munch. Let's say you're at a munch or other kink event, and you see two people engaging in a kink interaction even though you haven't seen them negotiate anything.

Maybe a submissive you're interested in approaches a third party and calls him 'Sir'. As a newbie, it's understandable to see this and believe she'll do the same for you. There might be a pre-negotiated relationship between these two that you're not aware of, or they may have been involved at some point, and she still calls him that out of respect. Don't ever assume anything. Like I said before, you'll likely just make yourself look like a twat.

Outside of basic respect, don't expect a damn thing from anyone you meet until you negotiate something with someone.

Before You Decide To Play With Someone

Remember that Communication is Key. Always.

Before you play, your need to communicate honestly with each other. Submissives and Dominants both need to have a good idea of what and what isn't going to work before you start a play session.

Submissives, please note: Your Dominant is not a bloody mind reader. They need to know what turns you on. So tell them. You might find it easier to do this by email, rather than face-to-face. However you tell them, you should be honest and specific. Do you love being spanked? Have you always wanted to try rope bondage? Do you absolutely hate needles? What if they suddenly produce some sharp needles while you're restrained? Don't hope your Dominant will guess these things—always tell them. Because if you don't, that's a good way to traumatise yourself, which will significantly limit your desire to explore other things you might very well enjoy.

Send your Dominant a few ideas of your own—the sort of things you would love to do. If it is practical and if your Dominant also likes the idea, it might happen. It might be fun.

On the day of your session, don't worry if you try something and don't like it much—that's totally allowed. Just be sure to share this with your Dominant. Likewise, if something works really well for you, say so. Your partner will love to hear that. And finally, always agree to and remember your safewords.

Remember that your agreement may change.

Agreements you set might vary, according to the setting or circumstances. You might have one set of rules for your primary partner, and another set for a casual play partner. You might have one set of rules for a discreet private scene, and another set for playing in public. So make sure you both understand and agree to any changes before beginning a new scene.

Remember to Stay Safe

Always play safely. If your Dominant pressures you into anything that you've already discussed as a hard limit, you're still not totally OK with it, walk away. If they drink alcohol before or during play, walk away. If you simply feel uncomfortable, walk away. Don't feel as if you've to go through with something if it doesn't feel right. I assure you that you most certainly do not.

And just to be clear, by 'walk away' I mean either don't start the play session, or immediately end it—not walk away from the relationship altogether.

I know that all this might seem a bit boring. Maybe you think taking the spontaneity out of a session will reduce the fun. But this is absolutely not so. When you know you're in safe hands, you can really let yourself go. If you like it rough, a good Dominant will be able to act convincingly, which will be much more fun than the real thing.

Chapter 7:

PLAYTIME

Now we've gotten to the part you've been waiting for. Playing with someone is a goal or milestone for everyone who is, or wants to be, involved in the BDSM lifestyle. It's also one of the most intimidating and easiest parts to screw up in this lifestyle as well. If you've been keeping up so far, that's awesome, and you should totally read on. But if you skipped the other chapters, I honestly suggest you go back and read them before you end up embarrassing yourself.

Now, I should tell you that nothing in this chapter (like all the others in this book) will tell you how to play with someone, or give scenarios, ideas, etc. That's not what this book was written for, and would remove the whole 'primer' aspect of the book. This chapter is about what you should understand and what you should expect from potential play partners and any play sessions you're involved in. Everything else will be left up to exploration on your part.

With that said, let's get started.

Let's Talk About Consent

First and foremost, I'm going to address consent. I mentioned this in Chapter 1, but it bears repeating: Consent is a HUGE factor in BDSM, and not going about it properly can really do some damage to you in ANY community. Now, consent as a concept has been widely employed in medical ethics over the years. So, unless you got into the scene before World War II, the word 'consent' has pretty much involved the same concept the whole time.

I've found that there are a lot of people involved in BDSM who arbitrarily toss the word consent into their sentences when talking about playing with someone, but don't really exercise anything that resembles consent. So let's take some time to clarify some of the things you should definitely understand about consent.

◇◇◇

Consent must be negotiated explicitly, where both parties demonstrate a clear understanding of the boundaries.

In some dungeons I've visited in the past, I've heard 'Well, so-and-so didn't know that the scene entailed (insert dodgy thing). No. HELL no. If they didn't know that beforehand, then that's a fail of the person in control of the scene.

Consent can be revoked at any time, for any reason.

Participants are not obligated to offer an explanation for their change in attitude towards an act.

Someone in an altered mental state cannot give consent.

If consent was given to do (insert dodgy thing) before playing, or the person was out of their mind, then that's fine. But if you're negotiating whilst a partner is in an altered mental space because of endorphins, then you're not getting consent, and it makes you a predatory dick.

Consent requires an understanding of the risks of the negotiated act.

'So-and-so didn't know what they were getting into' isn't an excuse; it's an explanation of how consent was not obtained.

Consent can be extended conditionally.

If one party consents to an act on the condition of reciprocation, and the other party doesn't make a reasonable effort to reciprocate, then the act is non-consensual. I've seen this come up a lot in offering aftercare and failing to follow through with play partners. Really, don't do that.

Coercion or intimidation undermines consent.

If emotional or physical coercion is used to establish consent, then it's not consent. The consenting party must feel that they are free to choose otherwise without unnecessary burden.

Consent doesn't dictate whether a scene was appropriate or acceptable.

Finally, having consent doesn't mean a Dominant can forgo good judgement in making decisions. Sometimes these judgements are quite subjective, and we do things more riskily than others, or these judgements don't go as planned. A Dominant has to take responsibility for those mistakes even if they had consent from their partner.

◇◇◇

BDSM Contracts

Before you begin any new D/s relationship, it's a good idea to have a contract. It spells out in detail what is expected of each person.

It also keeps things safe and consensual.

Even if you're married to the person and are starting to enjoy BDSM together, a contract can make communication easier. Plus, it's incredibly sexy to discuss sexual rewards and punishments with each other.

◇◇◇

What is a BDSM Contract, exactly?

It's a document/agreement within any kind of power exchange or BDSM play. More importantly, it's a useful way to open up the lines of communication and negotiate the terms of play. They can be as simple as a handwritten page, all the way to a ten-page document complete with legal jargon. Here are some things to keep in mind:

Your contract should be somewhat formal

As much as I hate using it as an example, I'm pretty sure that everyone has likely seen the Fifty Shades of Grey contract scene. In the movie, Anastasia and Christian amend the contract, discussing their hard and soft limits. It's done at his workplace, at an office table.

While your negotiations don't have to be this elaborate, they should definitely be more than just a conversation. There are (and should be) expectations that need to be discussed before entering into ANY dynamic of ANY type with anyone. If you're just talking about what you like and don't like in bed, you're basically having a regular vanilla discussion.

Why Have a Contract?

• They establish clear rules, boundaries, limits, punishments, etc.
• They define goals in the relationship
• They guide your relationship, whether short or long term
• They create moral authority

• They can extend the role-play aspect

Are BDSM Contracts Legal?

Despite what a lot of people seem to think, BDSM contracts are most certainly are NOT legal. I'm not even sure of where people got that idea in the first place, to be honest. 'Consensual slavery' isn't a legally binding thing. No matter what was negotiated on your contract, A Dominant can't take their submissive to court because they didn't suck your cock on a Wednesday, or they want to permanently stop things, and you want them to stay.

◇◇◇

Who's got the Power in a Power Exchange?

I've noticed that as BDSM evolves, there appears to be a lot more switching with newbies to this lifestyle. A lot of this comes from people who want to keep themselves guarded against people who might be predatory or just complete jackasses. Thus, there can be confusion as to who wields the power, especially with newbies. This was a question that was easy to answer in the previous generation's black and white approach of a D/s dynamic. While those thoughts still exist with a lot of people, it's a bit more complex now.

I think the actual power exchange is a two-stage process. You might have heard or read something akin to the submissive 'having the power' in a D/s relationship. This is totally true, but only in two areas of a D/s relationship—the negotiation phase and power exchange.

In the negotiation phase of the relationship, the submissive does indeed hold the power, in my opinion. The submissive is generally the one stating their hard limits, and has the power to reject what they don't want. This 'veto power' is, by its very nature, not submissive and can be a bit unsettling to a newer Dominant.

But as I am fond of telling submissives, 'Until you actually negotiate a D/s dynamic (no matter how basic), you are not anyone's submissive.'

Even if the submissive is unconsciously acting in a 'power positive' role by having the aforementioned veto power, I don't see any conflict here. It does nothing to reinforce the argument that, 'It is the submissive who has the power. At the negotiation stage, I would accept that the submissive might be in the power position. However, once we get to the second stage—the actual power exchange—the dynamic changes. And with it, the progression from kink to BDSM.

The Dominant is now given authority over a range of negotiated aspects of the submissive's life, from sexual to lifestyle aspects. The degree of this power varies from couple to couple, but the power is clearly in the hands of the Dominant at this point. It should be said that the power which remains with the submissive at this point is the power to end ties with the Dominant.

◇◇◇

When Play is No Longer Play

There seems to be this very misguided idea that it's totally acceptable for the Dominant partner in a relationship to participate in aggressive play when they are angry, so long as it is referred to as a scene or as being kinky. I'm going to let you know, if your Dominant is hurting you out of anger, that shit is fucking abuse.

A lot of newer submissives and slaves seem to think that this type of behaviour is permissive, so long as they feel that they have done something wrong. If one of your vanilla friends came to you and said that they had been rude to their partner and were then beaten or otherwise physically punished, would you be concerned? Of course, you would, because you would become immediately aware that your friend is dating an abuser. So why is it different when looking at BDSM?

Here's an example: A few years ago, someone mentioned to me that they should have known better than to be mouthy to her Dominant, because last time she did that, she had a massive beer bottle shoved inside her rectum.

She was mouthy—which, granted, she shouldn't have been—but the punishment given immediately put her life in danger. The anal cavity forms a vortex with things going into it, which is why nothing without a base should ever be inserted into the rectum, FYI. The pressure of the sphincter contracting can cause the bottle to shatter and tear the inside walls of the rectum, which are very close to a lot of important veins and arteries.

Her Dominant risked her life because she was mouthy. However, does that sound even the slightest bit reasonable? No, no, it doesn't. That guy was a fucking cock nozzle, and it pisses me off every time I think of it.

If you're now trying to justify beatings or something that is less obviously dangerous than this woman's case, then you're looking at this the wrong way. Even if the beating is administered in the same way it's administered during play, though physically safe, it's priming your mind for, and putting you in an abusive mindset.

Yes, there are punishments which can be quite physical in this lifestyle. A slap in the face to remind a submissive of their place within a scene, or not being allowed to shave their legs for a week, or a forced essay. But if your partner is actually angry at you, for any reason, they should not be laying a hand on you. There are no fucking instances in which this is remotely acceptable, because SSC isn't being followed.

Anger clouds judgement, which eliminates the sane element, just as alcohol or drugs do. When sanity is gone, there is a lack of safety occurring, and your life becomes in jeopardy because they are not trying to train you; they are simply beating you. And no matter how much of a pain slut or masochist you are, beatings, when you've messed up, are not consensual—they may ease your guilt if you come from an abusive background because you may feel that you have served your penance, but know that this is not a healthy response.

Establishing physically abusive routines is mental abuse, and it changes how you interact with your Dominant.

You shouldn't be walking on proverbial eggshells around your partner, or feel like you should be doing so. You should, of course, be striving to follow the rules established in your contract, and if physical punishments for misbehaviour are what you've established in your contract for your dynamic, that's totally fine—but these punishments can't or shouldn't happen in the heat of the moment when your partner is angry.

At the time of this writing, according to the National Sexual Violence Resource Center, 48% of women are emotionally abused in their lives, 42% of women are physically abused, and approximately 19–25% are sexually abused. Globally, around 30% of women experience physical and/or sexual abuse in their lifetime. Though not as frequently as women, men can be subject to abuse as well, with 49% being emotionally abused during their lives, 42% being physically abused, and around 7–30% being sexually abused.

Take precautions, and if you feel that you're in an abusive relationship, remember that no matter what, you don't have to take anyone's abusive behaviour or ever believe that you're supposed to take it, either. You can always leave, and there are resources available to help you do so.

Chapter 8:

RECOGNISING SUB-DROP

S ub-drop—also called submissive rebound—is a brief depression a submissive sometimes falls into after experiencing an intense play session. Sub-drop can appear in a lot of different ways, typically manifesting itself as feelings of depression, heightened anxiety and a sensation of 'distance' between the submissive and the Dominant. Sub-drop is a reaction that occurs in most submissives at some point in their relationship with a Dominant. It's typically more common in long-term relationships than in casual play encounters.

◇◇◇

So, what is sub-drop, exactly?

Technically, sub-drop is what happens to your body after you've drained your brain of all the hormones and chemicals that it releases from your brain during a scene or session. These chemicals include a release of epinephrine, as well as a dump of endorphins and enkephalins, producing the same effect as a morphine-like drug. This increases the pain tolerance of the submissive as the scene becomes more intense, and is typically the gateway to entering subspace.

Da fuk? That sounds bloody fantastic!
It is, actually. Those chemicals are why masochists do all the fun BDSM things they do. There's a high gained from the interaction, the intense intimacy, and the flood of all-natural drugs from those sessions. But, there's a bit of a problem. Lemme 'splain...

On a normal day, your body is dripping the aforementioned chemicals at a super low rate, with small dumps happening during exercise—if that's your thing. However, during a session, you can be flooded with them, and your body/brain can unfortunately only replace them at its normal rate.

There's no way to speed up the creation of all those chemicals, and it takes time to rebuild your store of them. If you happened to use a LOT of those chemicals, that's when sub-drop can come in. Sub-drop typically happens within forty-eight hours of a session, and it's a bit like drug withdrawal, unfortunately, with all the nasty consequences that come with it, and the feelings can last up to two weeks.

Well, that fucking sucks. So what does sub-drop feel like?
There are a lot of different ways sub-drop can show up. Physically speaking, it can show up as feeling like a hangover, or as if you stayed up too late (even if you got more than enough sleep), or you could wake up just feeling off-kilter. Emotionally speaking, feelings of loneliness, abandonment, mental exhaustion, confusion, insecurity, tremors and many other physical symptoms will be at their peak.

If you've had a pain session, then there's going to be the bruises, soreness, and pain from post-session fun, in addition to being tired. Now, regardless of what some books (typically erotica) will tell you,

you're not going to feel a normal spanking the next day. You'll be able to sit down just fine, seriously.

However, if your session involved caning, a whip, an intense rope tie, or anything the like, you're going to feel it and it's going to wear your energy down. Because your body is going to be short on the needed chemicals to give you a boost, this can make you crash and abruptly become exhausted, and being tired can make you emotional.

The emotional side of sub-drop is the more dangerous half. Emotions can wreak havoc on your logic. For example, you can go from being totally fine with your partner to suddenly feeling abandoned, depressed, or unloved. You might begin to see your partner's absence as a reflection of their 'true' opinion of you, and what your real worth or value to them might be.

These thoughts and feelings will seemingly come from nowhere and will likely surprise you.

I've been told on more than one occasion that the feelings have shown up whilst doing something mundane like ordering coffee, and then BOOM, the next moment they felt like they wanted to cry, or found themselves upset at their partners for a reason that seemed totally logical at that moment. This can happen with Top-drop as well. Believe me, I know.

Is there a way to avoid sub-drop?
There are definitely a few things you can do to avoid sub-drop. First, make sure you've eaten something before playing. Eating a light, high-protein, low-carbohydrate meal an hour or so before the scene can help ease a lot of symptoms. Just make sure to leave yourself enough time to properly digest your food before the session, and be sure not to overeat. Drinking plenty of water before and after a

session will help as well. A glass of something high in simple sugars, like orange juice, right after can help as well, to help your body rebalance as it recovers from the chemical crash.

Aftercare is an incredibly important thing after a session, and can definitely help in avoiding a drop. Let your Dominant take care of any marks you might have. Indulge in lots of warm and fuzzy physical touch to balance out all the kinky touching. Wrap yourself in a blanket to stay warm, get cuddled and snuggled and doted on. This will give you a lot of good things to remember, and you can think on those things if you begin to experience a drop.

Make sure you and your Dominant have talked about a follow-up and how this will be done. Will they call you? Text you? Will you be able to reach them if sub-drop happens? Communicate with them about the possibility of a drop and what the expectations are on both sides. If you don't have these set out beforehand, then that drop might suddenly make you upset or angry with them if they're unreachable. Another thing to be aware of is that not all Dominants give aftercare, so you've to be prepared to take care of yourself, if need be.

Evaluate, and communicate.
Text or call your partner as soon as humanly possible. A competent Dominant will know what sub-drop is, and be able to talk to you about what it is you're feeling, and why you're feeling it. However, if you can't get in touch with them, you need to stop and evaluate.

Remind yourself that sub-drop is normal, remind yourself of what happened during and after the session. There should have been aftercare, even if it happened quickly, or if it was a whole night of cuddling in bed together—think about how much your Dominant cares for you and appreciates the time you spend together in a scene. Sharing your experiences can lead to an even closer bonding with your partner, along with a deeper understanding of yourself.

Is there anything else I can do?

Sometimes, I've had my submissives prepare drop kits—especially for those moments when I couldn't be immediately available. Drop kits have always helped them if I wasn't immediately available, and I'm sure having one would help you as well. As far as what you would put in the kit, you know yourself better than anyone, so put those things that would make you feel better in your kit. A drop kit can be helpful for submissives and Dominants alike, and those who experience moderate to severe drop after play sessions.

Keep in mind that a drop can be associated with a lot of symptoms. It's very important to take care of yourself during times of sub-drop, and this kit will put all the things necessary to do that at your fingertips.

For example, you can keep a few caffeine shots, or bottles of 5-Hour Energy in your kit, which would help you're tired. Chemically speaking, these might help to provide a substitute for what your brain might actually provide if your body hadn't used up the ones it normally has.

If you're feeling a bit emotional, think of what things make you feel better when you're sick—because in a way, you are. A fuzzy blanket, bubble bath and music, sweets, a favourite drink or movie, etc. If you like to journal, keep a notebook with you to write out how you feel, getting the words out of your head and onto paper. This might also help you to clear your mind before you talk to your partner.

Like I mentioned before, not all Dominants give aftercare, or give sufficient aftercare for that matter—especially if it wasn't negotiated beforehand. Taking care of yourself after you play is a personal responsibility as well, so own up to it!

Drop Kit Checklist (For Submissives & Dominants)

Here are some ideas for what to include in your personal drop kit. Adjust based on what comforts you most.

- Fuzzy blanket or soft hoodie
- Favourite snacks or sweets
- 5-Hour Energy/caffeine shot
- A comforting drink (juice, tea, etc.)
- Journal and pen
- A printed or handwritten note to yourself from your Dominant or a past positive moment
- Comfort items (stuffed animal, stress ball, etc.)
- Small playlist of soothing or affirming songs
- Bubble bath sachets or calming essential oils
- A photo or reminder of aftercare from a past session
- Emergency contact or pre-written message to send to your Dominant

Customise your kit to suit your needs. You know what makes you feel safe, grounded, and seen—pack accordingly.

◇◇◇

Don't blame yourself.

Finally, the most important thing for you to remember is that while sub-drop may happen, you might be someone who frequently gets it, or someone who never does. If you happen to be someone on the frequent end, or you feel that something like it has happened, or is happening to you, like I said, it's totally normal, and just the natural reaction of your body to the loss of all those chemicals I mentioned before.

Don't be ashamed that you dropped. No matter how much experience you have, you may drop. Even if you haven't had sub-drop in years, a particularly intense scene could leave you feeling a bit off. It's okay. Just take care of yourself, keeping in mind that it's no one's fault. When you begin to level out those sensations and feelings will decrease and diminish, and you'll be back to normal and ready for more kinky fun in no time.

Chapter 9:

COLLARS

You've probably seen a BDSM collar, also called a bondage collar, and wondered what it is, what it means, and why people wear them. Or maybe you are considering a BDSM collar, and you want to make sure it's right for you.

◇◇◇

Not Just Jewellery

Before I continue, I want to say that collars are not a fashion statement and should be respected as such. It's a symbol of a type of deep commitment a submissive has with their Dominant. It serves as a reminder of the set of rules, guidelines and values a submissive must live by while they possess it. Being collared is a precious thing and should not be entered into lightly.

For many, wearing or giving a collar is emotional, sometimes intense. It's not just about power—it's about trust, visibility, and shared purpose.

For example, I've seen people give a collar to anyone ten seconds into their relationship, and then a week later, find that they're not even together anymore. Which is really freaking annoying, to say the least.

Based on what I've been taught, have experienced, and have witnessed, this isn't truly collaring someone. Collaring someone takes a significant amount of time, most of which depends on a lot of other factors that I can't go into. But I'll explain what I can.

◇◇◇

What is a Collar?

Simply put, a BDSM collar is a piece of jewellery with a secret meaning. Typically made of metal or leather, a collar is traditionally something worn about the neck of the submissive, like a necklace or a choker, to signify many things. Other types of jewellery worn in other places (such as anklets or bracelets) are also considered by a lot of people to be BDSM collars, but I've my thoughts on this.

I believe collars are best for those in the BDSM lifestyle. While there is indeed an evolution regarding the types of things worn as a collar, a lot of vanillas wear necklaces or other types of jewellery all the time, so wearing something similar would give no distinction between vanillas and a lifestyler.

Yes, I totally understand a submissive not necessarily wanting to out themselves. There are several things a submissive could wear around their neck that would be discreet enough to be worn publicly. A bracelet or ring will not have the same effect. Also, a collar has a different meaning than other types of jewellery.

A collar is not:

• a quick-accessory for sex play

- a 'gift' given without consent or discussion
- something to wear just because it looks edgy
- the same as a kink necklace

◇◇◇

A Little History

Collars in historical times were put on slaves to identify who owned them. To collar someone at the neck meant that you held that person in ultimate control. Today's purpose in the BDSM lifestyle community collars carry many different meanings depending on the individual, but generally speaking, the significance of the collar is the same: a person has control over another. One very important distinction from our historical counterpart rests in the consensual nature of the collar.

Collars were used as part of metal restraints in ancient times. For example, iron collars were used by the Romans to identify slaves and even give instructions for their return. It's likely that these historical practices led to the association of slavery with collars in subcultures like Old Guard leather and in BDSM fiction, such as the Story of O and the Gor series.

Gay leathermen traditionally used a padlocked chain to collar their slaves. A tradition developed in some leather bars in the 1980s of wearing a collar with an open padlock to indicate that one was seeking a partner, and a closed padlock to indicate that one was in a relationship. This symbolism became less common in the 1990s, as even in gay leather bars, many men began wearing collars for fashion purposes rather than indicating a relationship or the desire for one. Traditionally, the top owned the collar and locked it on his slave. Slaves or potential slaves did not collar themselves.

Today, BDSM collars range from the traditional leather look to stylish pendant necklaces and simple chains. You've probably seen a friend or co-worker wearing a discreet BDSM collar, without even knowing it.

The types of collars given to a submissive may take many shapes and can vary depending on the relationship, community, or several other factors. Typically, a Dominant will pick the collar out for their submissive. They may involve the submissive in the process, but normally the decision is ultimately the Dominant's.

I once met a submissive who told me the first time she wore her collar, she couldn't stop touching it—like it anchored her. 'It felt like being chosen,' she said. 'And I didn't take it off for weeks.'

◇◇◇

What Does a Collar Mean?

At its core, a collar signifies that the submissive wearing it is taken in some way—committed to or owned by a particular Dominant. It's a powerful symbol of connection, trust, and agreement within BDSM dynamics.

However, the BDSM community is rich with a vast and ever-growing array of identifications, labels, and meanings around collars. There are different types of collars—play collars, training collars, and formal collars—and each can carry different nuances depending on the people involved.

Because of this wide variety and the deeply personal nature of collar meanings, exploring every possible interpretation is beyond the scope of this book. Instead, I'll focus on some of the most common and widely understood meanings you're likely to encounter on your journey within the lifestyle.

For some couples, the collar is simply a sign of their relationship to the BDSM community—an outward symbol showing they belong to this world. For others, a collar can be more intimate: a sort of promise ring, representing a commitment between Dominant and submissive. Sometimes, a collar is as significant as a wedding ring, worn as a formal symbol of partnership. These collars are often presented by the Dominant to the submissive during a special Collaring Ceremony, which may or may not be part of a traditional wedding.

I've also seen plenty of people—usually newcomers—wearing collars as a personal statement that they're into BDSM, but without any particular relationship or dynamic behind it. As I mentioned earlier, a collar is not a fashion accessory or a casual statement. Wearing one without understanding or respect for its significance dilutes the true meaning—the sacredness—of what a collar represents in the dynamic between a Dominant and a submissive.

If you genuinely believe in and want to live by what most consider a 'true' BDSM lifestyle, it's essential to understand and honour the significance of a collar.

If you're curious about wearing or giving a collar, remember this: talk, listen, and learn first. Collars don't make a relationship—trust does.

Chapter 10:

TRUTHS AND MISCONCEPTIONS OF BDSM

Over the years, I've noticed that a lot of people involved in BDSM—both newcomers and longtime participants alike—carry some pretty big misconceptions about how BDSM relationships actually work. This is especially true when it comes to how submissives are supposed to be treated, respected, and valued within a healthy dynamic. Some of these misunderstandings come from certain stereotypes or fiction, which I'll get into in a moment, while others are fuelled by inexperience or poor examples in the community.

There's been this idea floating around that Dominants are meant to be harsh, distant, or constantly in control of every moment—and that submissives, by contrast, are meant to simply obey, without any definitive thought or question. That's not dominance; that's performance. And it doesn't reflect the depth or integrity of a real D/s dynamic.

If you've picked up some of these ideas along the way, they might already be affecting your relationships—or they could start to, down the line.

These are the kinds of things that come up a lot in conversations I've had with people in the scene. And while some of it might seem like common sense, let's be honest—when it comes to this lifestyle, it's better to hear something twice than to miss it entirely. You can never be too informed.

That's why I make a real effort to challenge these assumptions, especially when I'm talking to people who are just starting to explore this side of themselves. Whether they're nervous about their submissive desires or unsure how to lead as a Dominant, the same misunderstanding tends to show up: that power exchange is a one-way street.

But the truth is, it's not. Real BDSM is rooted in mutual care, responsibility, and trust. A Dominant leads with intention. A submissive offers themselves with discernment. Both roles require strength, self-awareness, and the ability to connect beyond surface-level fantasy.

Now, even though I'm focusing mainly on submissives here, these truths apply to anyone who wants to be part of a real BDSM dynamic. Whether you identify as Dominant or submissive, it's all relevant. So, let's get into it, shall we?

◇◇◇

Truths About BDSM

Truths about Living It

- You have rights. You've the right to walk away from your relationship at any time, for any reason. However, you should be honest and upfront with your partner when or if asked why. Because breakups fucking suck, and no one deserves to be left in the dark as to why they were broken up with.

- Living this 24/7 lifestyle is not a myth. However, living this lifestyle 24/7, whilst naked and kneeling in chains, is. No matter how bloody sexy that may sound, it's just fucking mad.

- No one can keep up a 24/7 high protocol lifestyle for long without a break for kids, family, work and other life events.

- At some point, you're going to have to take off the kinky clothes to go do real-life shit. It's a real thing that happens to adults, I've heard. Get used to it.

- An argument is not the end of the world. However, not resolving said argument might be.

Truths about Sex

- BDSM is not always about sex. It's totally fine to do vanilla shit. Seriously, find a damned hobby or something.

- There are going to be times when you don't feel like having sex. It does and will happen. Prepare yourself mentally for it because it's just a part of life and doesn't mean you're a bad submissive.

- You don't always have to be in the mood for sex, and it should be respected when you don't. There's a lot more to being in any relationship than sex, and if that's all your relationship seems to be, you should probably think about being in a different one.

- Ladies, there is such a thing as PMS, and no amount of dominance will make it go away. A competent partner, who gives a damn about you, will understand this. You reading this, guys?

- Unless you and your partner have been tested at least twice in the last year, or are really wanting a kid, then seriously—use a bloody condom. Because the reality is that people fall pregnant (and it's typically a surprise, unwanted, etc.), people get sick, and people die.

Truths about Other Lifestylers

- The people you meet are not always going to be nice, but they should be cordial, at the very least. People aren't always going to accept or understand your kinks, and they don't have to, either. Understand this, deal with it, and move on. This isn't secondary school. And if you're still holding on to a secondary school mentality, then you're not yet mature enough to involve yourself in this lifestyle.

- Just because their screen name says Dominant, Domme, Mistress, or Master—doesn't mean they are one. Or a competent one, at that. Nor should they ever treat you like you are their submissive, unless you've already reached that point in negotiation with them.

- Just because you call yourself a certain type of submissive or slave doesn't mean that others will agree with your definition (believe me, I disagree with people all the damned time). However, you should be prepared to defend your views, but don't get pissed off at others for their opinions. They have a right to them, just as you.

- No one will ever understand your collar and its meaning but you. Being proud to wear your collar everywhere is bloody fantastic, because it's a special thing to you, as well it should be. But showing it off at the local supermarket isn't—and it's rather tacky.

Truths about Dealing with Your Dominant

- Your Dominant doesn't always have their flogger nearby. Your Mistress is not always dressed in thigh-high boots and garters. Sometimes, joggers and a tea will be had.

- There will be times when you'll see your Dominant going through and stress over normal people things in their lives. Get over it—they're human. But they should never take their stress out on you. That's a form of abuse.

- While they may be intuitive, your Dominant is not a bloody mind reader. You need to be open and honest with your feelings about any matter. And you should expect the same of them.

- Don't walk away from your family or close friends for the sake of your Dominant. Because that's just fucking crazy, highly not recommended, and you should stay the hell away from anyone that would ask you to do such a thing because NO one is that awesome. Except for me, and even I would tell you not to do that.

- If you want something, ask. Be sure to ask respectfully, and ask with the understanding that your Dominant will make the best choice for you, so you may not get your way all the time. But definitely ask. Because if you don't, chances are, you're not going to get it.

◇◇◇

Misconceptions about BDSM

BDSM Relationships are Always Kinky

A lot of people believe that BDSM relationships need to have some sort of constant kink element to it, that all parties of the relationship need to be constantly playing and can't relate to 'normal love'. They believe that love is found in dealing with and receiving pain, or whatever their particular kink practice may be.

Wholeheartedly loving and caring for a submissive, wanting to make them as happy as possible and displaying this love in an affectionate manner, does NOT make one any less of a Dominant. In my experience, doing these things only strengthens the bond that I have with my submissives.

This way of thinking is an ever-present one in a lot of communities that I've interacted with, as I've found loads of people who believe that there are things that those in BDSM relationships shouldn't be doing—that vanilla love and practices are both taboo and humiliating—and this couldn't be further from the truth.

The truth is—and I'm sure most of you can agree—that at the end of the day, most people are still looking for love.

Dominants are Dangerous/Sadistic

While it's very true that most Dominants might enjoy having power over their submissive, everything is agreed upon upfront. BDSM relationships are (and should be) highly consensual, and competent Dominants are only going to practice something their submissive likes and enjoys.

A Dominatrix Hates Men

I don't think this is true for most Dominatrixes, to be honest. Because I can't speak from experience, I asked members of my house who happen to be Dominatrixes, if they hated men, and they all said no. They agreed that while they enjoy men's company and feel no hatred for them, dominating someone, whether male or female, was a bloody good feeling for them.

Submissives are Submissive in Every Aspect of Their Lives

Completely un-fucking-true. Many men or women who are dominant on a daily basis enjoy being submissive in BDSM. They could be CEO's of big corporations, with employees they are responsible for. Sometimes they have children or spouses and have a responsibility to take care of the family.

To become a submissive at least for the length of the BDSM experience—which could be just an hour or so—is considered a mental break or sex vacation. It's a moment when they can get rid of the pressure of constantly commanding, organising and managing the people around them. It's a form of relaxation, providing a sense of relief from the burden of being constantly responsible for others.

Being Submissive Is Humiliating

Submission only involves humiliation if that is what the practitioner desires. Some submissives want to be called names or made to do humiliating things, while others do not. Being submissive can be fun because the submissive person is receiving the pleasure they desire.

Even if a bottom does something humiliating during a session, the fantasy is temporary, and the inequality disappears after the session is over. This may be different for those submissives in 24/7 dynamics, but the humiliation they experience shouldn't be ongoing, as this is a form of abuse.

Men are always Dominants

Totally untrue! I've found that there are a lot of women who have submissive fantasies, but when it comes down to actually playing, there are loads of men who also want to take that role. Speaking from experience, as I had to act as a submissive for a time, I'll proudly say that it's not my thing. As a matter of fact, I fucking hated it. However, I know a LOT of men who would gladly fall under a Dominatrix.

BDSM techniques are always painful

BDSM doesn't only mean hurting someone, geez. There is SO much more to it than that. BDSM can be light and erotic, or involve role-playing, various fetishes, or other types of fantasies. You can play for hours without causing or receiving pain.

Domination Means Having Aggressive or Painful Sex

BDSM does not always include sex. And even still, it doesn't have to be some full-on jujitsu match if it does. Truth be told, the jujitsu thing actually sounds like it could be a lot of fun, but I digress.

There are a lot of BDSM practices that forbid sex, instead employing orgasm control, teasing and denial, chastity, or ruined orgasms.

Sometimes, a Dominant might allow a submissive to finally orgasm by masturbating, or command the submissive to orgasm at a later time. This is typically the case with most pro-dommes, as having sex with their clients is usually never an option.

People who like BDSM are bored or don't want regular sex

Nope, not true. Even BDSM practitioners sometimes like classic vanilla sex. While BDSM sessions are a fantastic alternative to in-the-bedroom, missionary position sex, they require a lot of work and preparation. However, to mix both BDSM and vanilla sex is a great way to keep your relationship fresh, and exploring your potential kinky sides just might bring a bit of mystery and desire back to your bedroom.

People who like BDSM are weird or sick

Well, yeah... That's the fun part. And we totally embrace it. All joking aside, there is unfortunately still a lot of social stigmas that surrounds BDSM. People assume that there must be something psychologically wrong with BDSM practitioners, that they must be suffering from anxiety, PTSD, depression, or have a history of sexual abuse. None of this is true. According to recent studies, we are, on average, happier, healthier, and open-minded—more so than our vanilla counterparts.

Chapter 11:

SEX TOY SHOPS YOU PROBABLY NEED TO CHECK OUT

I 'll be honest with you: I absolutely love sex toy shops.

For me, they're right up there with dungeons as some of the only places in the world where I feel completely at ease—where the world makes sense, and I don't have to filter or tone anything down. There's something about walking into a space unapologetically devoted to pleasure, curiosity, and kink that just feels right. No shame, no judgement. Just tools, ideas, and possibilities.

Over the years, I've had the chance to visit a fair number of these shops in my travels. Some were forgettable. A few were... let's say, questionable. But several stood out—not just because of their product selection, but because of the people running them, the energy in the space, or the sense of care and intention that went into the experience. Those are the ones that stuck with me. Those are the ones I want to tell you about.

Now, if you've ever had a conversation with me, you probably know that I happen to be a fairly private person. I don't share easily, and I tend to keep things close to my chest. But, as I'm fond of telling people, this lifestyle is also about connection, discovery, and trust—so I'm making a small offering here, before we close out this book.

What follows in the next few pages, is a list of sex toy shops I've personally found worthwhile. So, whether you're shopping for your first flogger or just want to explore places that take kink seriously and respectfully, I think that these shops are absolutely worth your time.

Go take a look. You might be surprised at what you find.

◇◇◇

M's—Tokyo, Japan

Located next to Akihabara Station in Tokyo, M's is a seven-story fun land, filled with adult videos, toys, and even used panties. Personally speaking, the best way to check out their shop is from the top down—like really nice cleavage.

The top three floors are all DVDs. Seriously, ALL THE DAMNED DVDs. Whatever your pervy heart can think of, you'll find it there.

On the fourth floor, you'll find all your cosplay-esque needs. I bought a couple of schoolgirl uniforms, which set me back about ¥3,500. On the third floor, you'll find two rooms of women's lingerie. It's not quite Agent Provocateur (another store you should check out), but it's pretty damned nice nonetheless.

All of the things you'd think would be in a sex shop are on floor two—vibrators and dildos, whips and masks, and a ton of ball gags.

And finally, on the first floor, it's all about fake vaginas and arseholes, with each one claiming to be the most realistic experience a penis could ever have.

The Pleasure Chest — USA
With five locations throughout the United States at the time of writing, which include stores in New York City, Los Angeles, and Chicago, The Pleasure Chest has made quite a name for itself as far as sex toy shops go.

I've visited the NYC locations and one of the Chicago locations. The stores all had a really classy look to them, which you'll notice as soon as you walk in. They also have a good selection of books, but they all seem to be geared toward women, because men don't read, I guess. I'm not a fan of novelty sex—well, anything to be honest—but if you're into that, then they sell those, too.

The staff in both locations were helpful and friendly across the board. So even if you're a newbie, you won't feel awkward at all. Some locations may not have everything you're looking for, but no worries—their website often has more, and they can usually order in what's missing from the shelves.

Lover's Lane — USA
Located primarily in the Midwest, Lover's Lane is one of those stores that are really good for newbies to BDSM or kink in general.

I've visited several locations throughout Chicago, and have found that most of them don't carry much that would do more than tickle more serious players, but some locations do sometimes have items that may indeed surprise you. Their stock can vary by location, and some shops carry a greater variety than others.

Generally, you'll find a lot of lingerie, light bondage gear, and playful toys aimed at couples exploring new territory. The atmosphere is usually bright, clean, and unintimidating, which makes it easy for first-timers to walk in without feeling overwhelmed. Staff are generally friendly, though knowledge levels vary—some associates can guide you through toy selection and offer useful advice, while others seem more focused on sales. If you're brand new to kink, it's a comfortable starting point. For seasoned players, it's more of a 'stop by if you're in the area' rather than a destination shop.

Adam & Eve—USA

Like Lover's Lane, North Carolina-based Adam and Eve is a really good sex toy shop for kinky newbies. The company sells just about any sex toy that you can think of—dildos, bondage, vibrators, cock rings, lingerie, lubes, oils and more.

With over sixty locations throughout the United States and Canada, you might want to have a visit if you're nearby. I'll let you know beforehand, they're a bit pricey in my opinion, but a great store nonetheless.

If you don't live near one of their retail locations, you can always check out the Adam and Eve website.

The Stockroom—Los Angeles, California, USA

I have no other way to say this—I LOVE this shop. The Stockroom is one of the oldest online sex toy shops in the world, and was honestly created with the BDSM community fully kept in mind.

I had a chance to visit their shop in Los Angeles, and while not overwhelming, I definitely felt like a kid in a candy store. From floggers to rope to chastity belts, this shop has more products than I can list, and if you're ready to take your toy bag from basic to badass, The Stockroom should be one of the first shops, if not THE first shop, you should check out. Believe me, you won't be disappointed.

If you're not able to visit their shop in LA (which is likely because they've only one shop), they pretty much have everything (and more) on their website.

Coco De Mer—London, England, UK

If the Marquis de Sade and Queen Elizabeth designed a sex shop, the result would likely be Coco de Mer. Founded by sisters Justine and Samantha Roddick—daughters of the woman who created The Body Shop— this place is hands down the classiest boutique I've ever had the pleasure of visiting. Their London shop oozes sophistication, and frankly, I wouldn't have expected anything less.

Coco de Mer is easily the most expensive sex toy shop on this list. It goes without saying that the shop sells some REALLY nice toys in their shop, vibrators, rulers, cuffs, floggers and more—most of which will have you mentally calculating how much your organs are worth on the black market. I spotted several pieces by Irish designer Paul Seville, which included some AWESOME leather-handled whips made with human hair. The best-seller? The redhead—because let's be honest, gingers are sexy.

Walking in feels like stepping into an erotic museum curated by royalty. If you can buy anything here without blinking, then we absolutely need to be friends.

Coco de Mer used to have locations in Los Angeles and Manhattan, but these days, their one and only shop is in London—so if you want the full decadent experience, you'll have to make the trip.

Harmony—London, England, UK

I think Harmony was one of the first sex toy shops that I ever visited. The 20-plus-year-old shop does a wide range of adult toys, underwear, magazines and videos. Harmony has a great selection of all sorts of things from leather, latex, rubber and PVC, as well as potions and lotions, dolls, couple kits and fetish items. Though not inexpensive, all the products are of pretty good quality.

The service can be a bit rubbish at times, but for the most part, the employees are nice and attentive. It's still one of my favourite sex shops—if only for the sake of nostalgia.

Harmony has two locations—one on Oxford Street and the other on Charing Cross Road. You should check them out if you're ever visiting and feeling a bit touristy.

Lovehoney—Online

Ah yes, 'the sexual happiness people'. Even though it's not a brick-and-mortar location, Lovehoney is still a great place to shop, which is why it's on my list of sex toy shops. They carry a ton of branded toys, as well as others.

While they are indeed a fantastic store, I have to tease them a bit for being the official licensor for Fifty Shades of Grey merchandise—purely in good fun, of course. You know I'm only kidding... mostly.

Twisted Monk — Online

If you want rope that feels like it was spun by angels with a minor fetish for perfection, Twisted Monk is where you go. Their hemp and bamboo ropes are a joy to handle—supple, smooth, and smelling faintly of the sort of craftsmanship that makes you want to coil it neatly and just... admire it. But that would be a terrible waste, because this rope is meant to be used. A lot. Twisted Monk's colour selection is gorgeous too, which is ideal if you want your scene to look as good as it feels.

They're a long-standing favourite in the kink community for a reason: they care about quality, they treat customers like humans, and they don't skimp on the details. The fact that they ship with care instructions is just the cherry on top. If rope bondage is your thing—or even if you're only rope-curious—this is the kind of gear you'll be smugly stroking while you tell friends, 'Oh, this? It's a Twisted Monk.'

Agreeable Agony — Online

Agreeable Agony's MFP rope is a bit of a different beast: strong, soft, and ready for heavy-duty play. It's got a slight slip to it—enough to make it easy to adjust mid-scene without tangling yourself into a pretzel, but still with the grip you need for secure ties. It's also low-maintenance and comes in a rainbow of colours, because apparently bondage can (and should) match your aesthetic.

This is rope that's built for players who want durability without the scratch or snag. It's ideal for those who tie often and want something that can stand up to repeated use without fraying, shedding, or turning into a sad, limp noodle after a few scenes. Agreeable Agony has a knack for making their gear practical without stripping away the fun—and that makes them worth checking out, whether you're a beginner or a seasoned rigger.

CONCLUSION

Hey there, I want to take a moment and say thank you for reading this book. I really tried to make sure that I gave you enough information about the BDSM lifestyle without totally overloading you with too much information, or boring the absolute piss out of you.

I hope you learnt new and/or valuable information from this book, and I hope it gave you a few things to think about. Even if it didn't, thank you for reading anyway. I encourage you to pass the book along to other like-minded people you know, and help them along their journey as well.

I'd like you to regard this book as just one point of view regarding BDSM. While I'd definitely like to think that my point of view is both a balanced and informed one, it's most certainly not the only point of view that exists, nor is it the only point of view I believe that any informed person—especially one involved in this lifestyle—wouldn't have eventually come to.

With this said, don't simply accept anybody as an authority. Be sure to check them out carefully, and make up your own mind as to their insight and whether you should be listening to them at all. Because there are some fucking idiots out there, let me tell you.

I wish you and your companions well in your explorations, and hope that I've helped to prepare you for your journey into the world of BDSM. Maybe we'll even meet at some point on said journey. If we do, there's definitely a drink to be had. Maybe a high-five or something. Hell, I don't know. We'll figure it out.

Anyway, good luck to you, and remember to be safe, keep your wits about you, be a positive part of your community, and try not to be a dick. Cheers.

ACKNOWLEDGEMENTS

This being my first book, there are a few people I want to personally say thank you to, because they all had a hand some way in my even writing the damned thing.

My heartfelt thanks to the elder members of my house for allowing me to write this book and trusting me to be a positive influence to our society and the communities in which we live. To my uncle, you're an awesome mentor, and I couldn't have asked for a better one. And to Amanda J, thank you for taking a chance on me when I barely had a clue. Thank you all for your faith in me.

To Abby M, thank you for your years of friendship, helping me make sure that I didn't completely lose my mind whilst constantly losing sleep, and for suggesting that I write this book. You're bloody fantastic for it. To Maria, thank you for being one of the most real people I know, for being one of my biggest advocates, and for telling virtually any kinkster within earshot to buy my book. It honestly means a lot to me, and I'm glad to know that people like you still exist. And to Veronica P, thanks for being one of the most amazing muses I've ever had. It helped me a lot more than you'd believe. You'll always be the Pepper Potts to my Tony Stark.

To other members of the communities I've been part of in some way, listed alphabetically: Adam P, Alecks, Alex, Alice, Amanda B., Arielle, Asha, Bad Hatter, Badm3l, Brother Bart, Becky, Ben, Betty, Bobby T, Bradley C, Brandon, Bruce Esinem, Caressa, Carly, Cassandra, Caramell, Cece, Chloe, CoolCat, Chris, Craig, Dan, Daemon Danes, Daydreamer, The Dereks, Deena, Erika M, Erika Y., Erin, Fatima, Foxy, Freja, Fulgrim, Gabby, Geana S. George, Gwenn, Heather R, Helena, Hulk, Jason, Jade, Jen, Jerith, Jerome, Jessica N, Jessie H., John, Jonathan, Joyce, Kane, Karen, Kay, Kimberli K, Kyle, Lady J Mayhem, Laura, Lea, LeatherRedux,

Marina, Matt, Mike, Miyoko, Ms. R3d, Munson, Monica, Mr. Mayhem, Nicole A, Razzberri, Ms Renard, Rick, Riotess, Ronin, Rubber-T, Madilynn, Padraic, Parth, Peter, PhukPuppet, Prty Demi, Roshi, Sara, Scott, Sebastian, Sin, TanningChatum, The Professor, Vitrify, Windy, Wolf, and Wilson.

Now, some people are going to (correctly) notice that they're not being shown proper gratitude here, or were totally forgotten. I'd like to apologise for that. Please contact me, and I'll fix that in future editions.

I am especially grateful to all of the fans of Dominant Desires, especially to the following people: Amber P, Rachael N, Genie S, Michelle C, Dominique L., Sal N., Naomi R, Amber N., Ana R., Khlee, Teddy, ArcticWoman, Stephanie R, and Angela L.

And finally, to seventeen-year-old Rajan... Good job getting off your arse, lad. By the way, you lose your hair.

R

ABOUT THE AUTHOR

Rajan Dominari has been part of the BDSM lifestyle for over two decades. He's a respected educator, speaker, and consultant whose work is rooted in lived experience—not borrowed theory.

In 2012, Rajan launched the blog Dominant Desires, offering sharp insight into power dynamics, masculine leadership, and the unspoken structure of D/s relationships. Since then, his writing has reached tens of thousands through essays and private mentorship.

He writes not for tourists, but for those with skin in the game. For those living this life, or learning it with honour.

Originally from London, England, Rajan now lives in Chicago, IL. He can often be found drinking a strong gin and tonic, thinking in silence, or imagining the sound of a flogger landing just right.

If Welcome to the Darkside helped you
find your footing,

For Those Who Know
will test your stance.

This is not a guide. It is a reckoning.
A collection of sharp-edged truths for those who
don't just practise power—but carry it.

For the Dominants who lead with honour.
For the submissives who yield with purpose.

For those who understand that obedience, control,
devotion—are never games.

For Those Who Know doesn't teach.
It reminds.

Available now from Raven Row Press